THE WORLD THAT
BELONGS TO US

THE WORLD THAT BELONGS TO US

An Anthology of Queer Poetry
from South Asia

Edited by

ADITI ANGIRAS & AKHIL KATYAL

HarperCollins *Publishers* India

First published in India in hardback in 2020 by
HarperCollins *Publishers*
A-75, Sector 57, Noida, Uttar Pradesh 201301, India
www.harpercollins.co.in

2 4 6 8 10 9 7 5 3 1

P-ISBN: 978-93-5357-457-4
E-ISBN: 978-93-5357-458-1

Typeset in 11/16 Adobe Jenson Pro at
Manipal Technologies Limited, Manipal

Printed and bound at
Thomson Press (India) Ltd

CONTENTS

PREFACE

February 2018. Travelling back from our first meeting at the publisher's office in Noida, on the e-rickshaw ride to the Botanical Garden metro station, we were both damn nervous but obviously excited. We had taken on something far bigger than ourselves, but had we also taken on something more than we could chew? We were not sure. The next several months would make us realize both the scope of our ambition but also the enormous weight of our task. And its (misplaced) temerity.

Next month, when we prepared the call for the anthology, we were quite unprepared for the long, collective life it would acquire. Folks circulated it online, emailed it to their friends, copied it on Facebook groups, WhatsApped it to their lovers, tagged their allies, acquaintances, and crushes, and gave us suggestions to add to it and edit it. So much so that the text of the call grew haphazardly as it circulated, taking stock of what its readers wanted it to be. With each share, the call kept expanding and growing limbs, each comment added its own voice and language to it. It evolved from what we thought it could be to incorporate, in some measure, what its readers wanted it to be. Even before the book started taking form, the readers, the contributors and the 'community' at large helped us sketch its outline.

In that long text of the call, we had invited entries from 'Transmen, Transwomen, Lesbian, Hijra, Kothi, Gay, Aravani, Khawaja Sara, Intersex, Jogappa, Bisexual, Drag King/Queen, GenderQueer, Non-Binary, Meyeli Chele, Butch, Femme ... and other poets'. We uploaded it happily, thinking the first task was done. MM chided us gently on the Facebook comment thread, saying, 'Not from asexuals?' We realized our mistake and added it immediately. PB commented, 'Uhm ... Pansexuals?'. AS said, '... how about the diaspora?'. 'Allies' wanted to know 'Can I also write?'. We said yes, of course, absolutely, but also realizing that the 'task' of putting together an anthogology of queer poems wasn't going to be self-evident.

Activist Ramki L. Ramakrishnan, from Chennai, suggested to us to add 'nupi maanbi and nupa maanba'. When Santa Khurai, a nupi maanbi activist and writer from Manipur sent us her poems, she put it clearly on record that '[p]lease do not identify me as Indian transwoman or a northeast transwoman. Please use: indigenous Meetei transwoman from Manipur to stand for nupi maanbi, in case the need arises.' Her email made it evident that our editorial fantasies of us knowing what we were doing needed some tempering. Open your eyes and ears, folks were saying to us. You have got started onto this, don't pretend to be all-knowing, have some humility, keep going.

Meanwhile, another activist prodded us to add 'Thirunangai' to the call. So, you see, it didn't remain a little exercise any longer between two little poets in Delhi. People made us share it and took work on themselves. They lent their hands on deck. They knew that we desperately needed them. They adopted the call in various measures, with love and solidarity, and even scepticism, and made it work for themselves, to various degrees. It also told us, yet again, that the word 'queer' itself is a little, little thing. It does only so much of the work and no more. It is a net editor-types usually like to cast but folks are not always waiting to be caught within it.

Which is why we had chosen to break up this part-weird, part-convenient, part-phantasmatic word 'queer'. We let it disperse. We made it splinter. Because this thing many of us know as 'queer' was only an odd, lovely but tentative bridge between us and for all the entries that would come to us in the coming months. People live their lives through a maddeningly complex slew of names, identities and gestures. 'Queer' only pretends to signpost them all, but it is precisely that, a convenient pretence, meant for book covers, not for all its contents.

Meanwhile, our friends translated the call into other South Asian languages. It went out in Malayalam, Tamil, Kannada, Gujarati, Hindi and Urdu. Apart from the English one. It should have gone out into many more languages but that's what we could manage in those early months. Anthologizing is a strange act. It makes you ambitious but also puts you in your place. As we went on with the task, we were realizing both the possibilities and the constraints of the city we lived in, the languages we were familiar with and hopelessly unfamiliar with, the 'circuits' we moved about in, which were multiple but nowhere as multiple as they should have been. At the beginning of the process, we were afraid that some of our constraints would become the constraints of this book. Some of those fears have been allayed. Others remained.

Entries had started to pour in. As this book goes to print, almost eighteen months after our call was published online, a few entries continue to trickle in. We received submissions from Bangalore, Baroda, Benares, Boston, Chennai, Colombo, Delhi, Dhaka, Dublin, Kathmandu, Lahore, London, Karachi, New York City, among many, many others. From the moment the book was conceptualized till now, it's been almost two years. As it stands, *The World That Belongs to Us* has more than a hundred contributors, poets and those who translated their poems. The poems are finally printed in English but have originated in more than ten languages, including Bengali, English, Gujarati, Hindi, Kannada, Punjabi, Malayalam, Marathi, Nepali and Urdu. Our translators have helped us understand these poems, both their larger contexts and their granular meanings. One poem seems to have escaped this exercise. All attempts to translate Shakti Milan Sharma's 'Laga Jockey Main Daag', seemed like betraying it. It refused to be rinsed of its original form. It is a Hinglish poem and is printed as such, using two scripts.

The editorial process was itself a slightly crazy task, both for us and for several of the contributors. Over those two years, for about half of the contributors, we had email threads, WhatsApp messages and calls of various lengths and intensities, to finalize the text of the poems. Where a translator was involved, the threads were triangular. Several poets were going to print for the first or second time, several did not see themselves as *writer-writers*; the edits were sometimes minor, sometimes more than minor.

From the conception of the project, we wanted to reach out to a diverse set of contributors. In terms of language, region, caste, gender, sexuality, class and individual publication history. We wanted to make space for first-time poets, to let this book be home not only to established queer English poets from South Asia (we're thrilled that they're also in our book, Kazim Ali, Hoshang Merchant, Ruth Vanita, Rajiv Mohabir, Minal Hajratwala and Vikram Seth, among several others) but we wanted this book to be owned by a larger, a more heterogenous set of queer writers and readers from South Asia. We were also keen to let our contributors know that if they choose to remain anonymous or use pseudonyms for this book, we'd welcome that. Several have exercised that option, indicating the tricky lives we live, ones full of negotiations, big and small.

As the entries came in, we were startled by the range of forms and subject matters that our fellow queer poets experimented with. The themes ranged from desire and loneliness, sexual intimacy and struggles, caste and language, body and gender, activism both on the streets and in homes, the role of family (both given and chosen), and heartbreaks and heartjoins. Some of the titles of these poems depict that – 'The Sonneteer Gets a Heartbreaker's Haircut', 'My Sister Takes a Long Long Time to Die', 'Resistance Rap', 'my high school nemesis finds me on instagram

& messages saying *oh shit S, you still like, a fucking lesbo?*', 'A bottle of whiskey and a knife in my backpack', 'La pulsion de mort', 'Should I mourn a little longer?' and 'Parliaments on the stoop'. The poetic forms chosen by the poets – free-verse, ghazals, sonnets, natty little rhymed numbers, list-poems, multilingual poems, prose poems, among others – carry the weight and ferocity both of their fantasies and failures in love, politics and often tricky journeys of the self that queer people make.

Then there was that other sword hanging over us like it hangs over most anthologists' necks. The question of 'quality'. In that first meeting we had with folks at HarperCollins in their Noida office, the word had made several guest appearances in our conversation, and all of us had nodded our heads in puppet-like unison. Yes 'quality', of course, 'quality'. The word was a talisman.

But when the process took off, we realized that the talisman was leaking from between our fingers. We no longer knew what we meant by it. What is a 'good poem', after all? That which plumbs the depths of our feelings, and brings back to the surface something we always recognized but hadn't been able to articulate in those serendipitously precise words? That which is 'layered' and 'nuanced' and 'complex' – those much used and abused classroom terms? That which makes the familiar unfamiliar to us, or vice-versa? That which opens up a world you hadn't felt intimately before, or not even chanced upon? That which is able to create community on being read, which sends out threads of fellow-feeling to many of its readers? What among these is the right answer? Is there one?

This good-ness of a poem itself is a jumpy thing. You can't tell if it lies within the poem or in the perceptions of the people outside it. Surely the social worlds, the cultural clout, the linguistic position of the readers inflects their understanding of this good-ness. And if the editors select only those poems which will pass the narrow test of 'quality', surely they are imposing not only their 'taste', but also the social and cultural foundations which moor it? And we know 'taste' (or its close friend 'merit') in South Asia is a loaded thing. It replicates social hierarchy. It unhears caste. And class. It pretends cultural capital does not exist. It ignores linguistic diversity and odd hierarchies which creep in between languages. It is not able to digest that each poem has an echo and a vagitus, each of it is a conversation, a meditation, a quarrel. Which different readers are poised to hear differently. So, for the question that we had arrived at – is there something imminent in the poem that makes it 'good' or 'bad' – our answers were no longer sure. The anthology has been produced with this uncertainty dancing in the middle of the room, rather than sitting quietly in the corner.

There was, of course, an allied question. What is a 'queer poem'? Years ago, when one of us had posed a similar question to Hoshang Merchant, editor of *Yaraana: Gay Writing from India* that came out in the late 90s, he had given us a series of answers, some of which contradicted each other. Anthologists never have the confidence of their cover pages. Not even half of it. Is a queer poem written by a queer-identified person about 'queer' themes, whatever those maybe? Can a non-queer person not address those themes as well, in a persuasive manner? Can a queer person writing about cooking or Mars or landlords or taking a dump in the morning also qualify as a queer poem? After all these are all also dimensions of a life of that person. Or do only themes of protest, anger, love, loss, gender, loneliness, body, joy, sexuality, law, social change, desire qualify as queer poems? We have had different answers to these questions at different points. 'Queer' turned out to be both an embodied experience available to some people but also a disembodied stance towards the world wielded by many. Mostly, we have erred on the side of being catholic in our choices, of including rather than excluding.

The fetishizing of the word 'queer' also meant that we lost out on stuff. When folks think the word means too little, they keep out of it. In keeping out of it, they thin out its story. When we asked the estate of a prominent poet to let us include three of their poems in our anthology, we received kind but firm regrets. 'For a variety of reasons,' the estate wrote back to us politely, 'we are not approving your request for any of the poems to be included in your collection.'

A 'variety of reasons' is a disarming phrase. You cannot argue with that. But our hunch is that the 'queerness' of the anthology had something to do with it. It is a magic word – queer. It creates invisible boundaries around it. When it doesn't, then others create those boundaries for it. To tell the word what it is not, what it cannot include, what it can long for but will lose out on. What was E.M. Forster's phrase in that last paragraph of *A Passage to India*? '... they said in their hundred voices, "No, not yet," and the sky said, "No, not there."' Another queer anthology in the future will have you. For now, we have left a single page blank as a tribute. *Yes, the world is still full of paper. There's enough missing for us to know you.*

The third set of questions for us were about the 'public' that a queer poem can form around itself. A public, i.e., the collective of people contributing, reading and engaging with this anthology. We were keen to know what forms of 'public' can accrue around a poetry anthology, specifically a queer one being published in South Asia. Reasons that expanded and contracted this mass of people did not always have to do with gender and sexuality. A Tamil poet, who we really wanted to include in the anthology, did kindly consider our offer but finally chose not to be a part of it. '[A]s much as we want diverse queer writings to be published by big publishers,' they wrote to us, 'we also are working to address the pay inequality in the literary space ... It is a tough and complicated decision to make. At this point we do not want to proceed. Hope you understand.' This anthology went through a moment like this and we want to put it on record. Where the field of its potential contributors contracted, rather than expanded, because of the terms on offer. The publishers had their version, of course, which was largely about mainstream English poetry publishing in India, and how it is an 'inherently stringent and resource-wise limited sphere' which they have to work with. But in all of this, we couldn't manage to include their voice. This is also the real-time limitation of the 'publics' an anthology can form. A future anthology will hopefully figure this out.

As the book stands, it has created its own complicated forms of public. Several of its contributors are *card-carrying queers* as it were, who have held placards, knocked on courts, questioned policemen, others have more tentative, quieter, more tangential relationships to words that say something about their gender and their sexuality. While most of our contributors have used their names for this book, some have chosen to remain anonymous, others have used pen-names, some of which were devised for this volume. 'It's complicated' turned out to be a close-cousin of living as a queer person in South Asia (not for all, but for many) as is true for many other parts of the world. We swim in-and-out of proverbial *closets* (that old, inconvenient image, as if our world can be parcelled into easy insides and outsides), sometimes incognito, sometimes staying overnight at an ally's home or using a friend's letterbox. We wear two, three, four sort of shoes to walk on all the tracks of our lives. The anthology got us proximate to these many shapes that queer lives take. Some author bios eschewed identity altogether (and why not), others foregrounded them. Some delivery addresses for the contributor-copies were the same as places where family members or landlords could see the package, others were not. There were existential email exchanges, and phone calls to discuss identity crises of many sorts, queer politics, editorial delay(!) and punctuation. We learnt from each of these conversations. Hopefully our contributors got something out of them too.

PREFACE

The title *The World That Belongs to Us: An Anthology of Queer Poetry from South Asia* had come to us in the first two minutes of discussion and just stuck around long enough to grow on us. Hopefully the book will grow on you. Our call had sailed to many shores. These poems are the messages we received in glass bottles, from near and far, from those we knew and those we didn't. From the 'well-known' to those whose poems so far could only be found in secret notebooks and ephemeral tissue-papers. What they sent us has an explosive diversity of themes. And of forms. Yet this is a *small* book. It has come at a moment in history. There have been others before it that broke new ground. There will be others after it, which will fill its gaps. Hope it has something to give you which you will cherish.

Aditi Angiras

Akhil Katyal

October 2019

New Delhi

ASAD ALVI

Asad Alvi's work has appeared in *We Will Be Shelter: An Anthology of Contemporary Feminist Poetry* (2014) and *Uprooted: An Anthology of Gender and Illness* (2015), as well as Columbia University's *Journal of Art & Literature, The International Gallerie, Kashmir Lit, Papercuts,* and *Dawn,* amidst others. They live in Lahore.

La pulsion de mort

'ab yahāñ koī nahīñ' koī nahīñ aa.egā', words
curling up like rings of smoke. Bathroom floor.
Faiz playing on the radio. I have filled my pockets with stones.
There is a river nearby. The Bisnumati. I am in Kathmandu. It is
2016.
I have run away from home, after a history of violence.
And I broke up
with the only boy who will ever love me: every time he kissed
my hips

      my scars became flames.
      'ab yahāñ koī nahīñ' koī nahīñ aa.egā'

yahāñ: this unvisited body.

It is the impossibility of queer love, the scholars say.
For whom the only future carved out is death.

For example, Williams, Tennessee. It is 1983.
He is discovered dead in his hotel room, a cigarette
hanging loosely from the lips, a note addressed to Robert.

or 1941:

Virginia's body at the bottom of the river, the stones
still in her pocket. Her love for Vita undeclared.
    'ab yahāñ koī nahīñ' koī nahīñ aa.egā'

RUTH VANITA

Ruth Vanita, raised and educated entirely in India, taught at Delhi University and was founding co-editor of *Manushi*. She is the author of many books, including *Love's Rite: Same-Sex Marriage in India* and *A Play of Light: Selected Poems*. Her novel, a lesbian romance set in eighteenth-century Lucknow, will appear in 2020.

Garment

Will it stretch that far? Will it go round three
Continents or four, three hearts or more,
And still slide through a ring?
Worn and unravelled night and day without
A break, past two time zones, retain
Its sleek, original shape?
How many machines can we put it through,
How many phones, planes, taped voices
And still find it wearable?
Is our love elastic, or some finer,
clinging, skinlike, inward-breathing weave
To make all this bearable?

After

I want to do the things we've done before
Unwrap you like a tall golden candle,
Light you, and drink the hot wax running down,
Drop, tangled in your arms, onto the floor.
I want to do the things we've never done.

Oh ask, this once, not for less, but more
Burn me like your candle at both ends
Take me by the clear light of the sun
Let us forget, again, to lock the door.
Let's do the things we thought could not be done.

SHALS MAHAJAN

Shals Mahajan is a writer, activist, layabout, part feline, somewhat hooman, genderqueer queer feminist fellow who lives in Bombay, but mainly in their head. They have been part of *LABIA – Queer Feminist LBT Collective* for the past two decades and their published works include *Timmi in Tangles*, *Timmi and Rizu* and *No Outlaws in the Gender Galaxy*.

I Swear

I swear I'd be kinky if I had panes on my face.
You know, the kind of face that can look austere,
and cold,
and flattened,
with intriguing hollows.

I swear I'd be kinky, no more,
    I'd be a dominant
if I could just look like that.

I'd stand in half-lit rooms,
    no, passages actually,
my arms would lie loosely by my sides,
    and still.
My fingers curled just so,
    a bit inside.

You couldn't discern any tremor if you tried,
or even, if you scrutinized.

Only my unblinking eye would give away
the fact that I was...

What's that word I am looking for?
Taut? Not relaxed? Quivering inside?
Nah.
            No quivers for me
            if I were standing like that...

You'd know that my shoulders were
stretched, like the wires of
some fine instrument.
Ready to play.
Precise
sharp
and clear.

That's the other thing.

I swear I'd be kinky if I had focus
and didn't get betrayed by my
constantly meandering attention.
By lanes, and slip lanes,
and sideways,
and laughter,
none of that steady,

steadfast (what a befitting word)
discontent.

I swear I'd be kinky
and a dominant
if I exercised regularly.

That thing about discipline, you know.
And that other thing about taut muscles.

Do you have any idea how tiring it is
to stay focused, discontent, troubled
yet peaceful, and taut?
My belly jiggles, alternating between laughter and tiredness.

And that's the other thing.
How does one stay focused on a role?
How does one stay focused in one space?
At one pace?
Or vary it, but just so?

How does one not wander off?
Or tell a joke?
Or start feeling gassy right in the middle of a stroke?
Or worse still, start giggling, at the absurdity of the pose?

Dammit!
These are tough things.
And I, a lazy bum.

I think I need to read my guide, some more.

A bottle of whiskey and a knife in my backpack

(for Bina)

Last night, in despair, you remind me of her novel.
A cataclysmic ending,
that seems closer today than ever before.

And as I write stodgy sentences this morning
her Narmada will not let me be.

I stand a few minutes in front
of the overcrowded cupboard,
and unerringly pull out,
the folder with the first draft of her novel.

I haven't read it in over a decade,
perhaps closer to two.
Has she been dead a decade already?
Can it be that long?

My lament of those years
'We were never able to retrieve
that final draft of her novel
after she died...'
is sludgy in my mind today.

I miss her. Her words –
sharp, fiery, and so right.
I just cannot lament any more.

That time has gone
and perhaps
it is not so terrible
after all, that she is not here.

She was always the irrational witness.
Could never keep her distance.
Be safe.

Falling. Falling deep
in to the abyss of every horror
and then, sending frail
smoke alarms
screams wails.

As if our ears were already not buried
in the cacophony of pain.
As if we could not tell
one scream from the other.
As if we needed her to tell us
how painful the scars were,
how little skin was left,
how much was lost, broken.

Yet, and again,
we formed a chain,
reaching to them,
and to her.

Her.

Night, after night,
of drunken lost phone calls,
from a dry state
of a heartless land.

Our distance protected us.
Our distance deprived us.

I remember most,
from those hours
of talking and crying,
holding the MTNL rotary phone
and sitting silently,
hearing you finally fall asleep.
Listening to the unnerving
rattle of your smoke
blackened lungs,
and falling asleep myself.

After all those threats
you did not, after all,
commit suicide.

Maybe if you had, you'd have planned your death better.
Left the final draft of the novel with someone who'd have cared.

You caught pneumonia,
promised to be back from the hospital
in a couple of days,
and were gone.

Leaving us blinking in shock and surprise
till we were able to gather ourselves,
across cities,
and get back to those damn phones.

Till the hugs and the holding
and the inevitable story telling
made us feel you were still
smoking amongst us.

Voices raised in song,
remembering the first one
I sang with you.

1995. Jaipur Conference.
The year I discovered
feminist euphoria, solidarity.
Fell in trance like love with every
other woman I met, so radiant,
so powerful, so articulate,
you all seemed.

'*Ho gayi hai peer parvat si, pighalni chahiye*
Is himalay se koi ganga nikalni chahiye.'

At night, finding the despair and pain of this song
with you, knowing that there was space for everything here.

I knew then that I'd learn about love like I could not have imagined.
And I did.

Bina, I am reaching that place today
where I begin to wonder
whether you did not have it right all along.

Despite our best efforts,
in every place you found yourself,
you snuck in a bottle of whiskey
and a knife into your backpack.

I wonder if this is all we too have left?

But I am still writing,
so I think I'll hang on a little while longer,
hoping that one day,
when the bottle has produced the knife,
someone will listen to me sleep,
and find the place to sleep too.

VIKRAM SETH

Vikram Seth is the author of three novels: *The Golden Gate*, *An Equal Music* and *A Suitable Boy*. He is also the author of several poetry collections, an opera libretto and two works of non-fiction, *From Heaven Lake* and *Two Lives*.

Across

Across these miles I wish you well.
May nothing haunt your heart but sleep.
May you not sense what I don't tell.
May you not dream, or doubt, or weep.
May what my pen this peaceless day
Writes on this page not reach your view
Till its deferred print lets you say
It speaks to someone else than you.

All You Who Sleep Tonight

All you who sleep tonight
Far from the ones you love,
No hands to left or right,
And emptiness above –
Know that you aren't alone.
The whole world shares your tears,
Some for two nights or one,
And some for all their years.

RAJIV MOHABIR

Rajiv Mohabir is the author of *The Cowherd's Son* (Tupelo Press 2017), *The Taxidermist's Cut* (Four Way Books 2016), and translator of *I Even Regret Night: Holi Songs of Demerara* (Kaya Press 2019). Currently he is an assistant professor of poetry at Emerson College and translations editor at Waxwing Journal.

Inside the Belly

I

The seaman James Bartley screams as he slides down a sperm whale's throat in 1891. He was in the stomach for fifteen hours, unconscious in the stench of digesting fish. He survived after his shipmates sliced the belly open and pulled his twitching body into bed, where he stayed for almost a month.

(If this happened today he would take seventy selfies and post them online.)

According to the tales, he lost his sight and his skin whitened. He wasn't holding any blade.

II
A black-swallower can take a man twice as big as himself, his jaws
    distensible.

Catching them by the tail, he walks them over to his mouth.

This is the marine-biology of deadly desire.

By most imperial standards in 1891 by the British East India
    Company my biology is a metaphor for black.

I am black-skinned.

As a child I prayed to be white until my foreskin started to whiten.

This is not the deep sea so spotting men is not impossible.

The internet is a type of black-swallower too.

III
A humpback hums as it tongues me. He doesn't spit me out after I
come in his mouth. I want to shed my skin for a white coat. I ride
him into the dark cold water of an unnamed sea. His flanks toss me
from the bow, make the scales fall from my eyes.

IV

According to the Royal College of Surgeons, any mating is a death wish.

A wish for whiteness is every white man you bed.

Consider the bull shark that swallows a blowfish whole or why you
    refresh your screen with the 'Load More Guys' feature on the app.

When it reaches the stomach it endures the acid and inflates before
    chewing through the shark's stomach lining.

Kippling's sailor placed a grating in the whale's throat to protect
    it from STIs but you like to cast cowries – stomach acid kills
    everything.

Your stomach still lurches with each tri-tone ring: which white man
    will you invite inside tonight, let erase you slowly?

Interpreting Behaviors

bina jawab barah saal se bulawat hai…
jane ki koi nahi sunal

Today scientists take interest in the things
that do not occur with equal frequency.

For example: why doesn't the only other
brown fag on O'ahu text after you harpoon

each other at Lē'ahi Park? Does his tail slap
mean to silence your calls when you say, 'we're one species'?

You swallow a sea of krill and upside-down, sing
the Sindhi folksong he taught you: *When the British*

sailed what weakness did they leave? Does he mean
your connection was one-sided like Kimiko's whale

crooning at 52 Hz, the only of his kind
who can sing his poetry to you in Hindi?

> *For twelve years he's been calling out to no response…*
> *That it knew no others listened –*
> -from Kimiko Hahn's 'Ode to 52 Hz'

GEE SEMMALAR

Gee Semmalar is a queer trans man from Kerala who is an activist, educator, theatre artist and filmmaker. He is interested in exploring the politics of identity, allyship/solidarity and intersectional discourses between caste, gender, race, sexuality and citizenship.

Resistance Rap

An Indian scientist
works overtime
in a Third World lab.
Dragonflies in glass cases
transform into technical experts
for the US military
to perfect drones,
sent to rescue Iraq.

They call it peace building.

A Colombian drug lord,
high on cocaine from Peru,
marked out to be shot
just fifteen minutes later,

goes down on his knees
to propose to his 14-year-old Lolita
with a diamond
found in Angola
and cut in Surat.

Isn't globalisation romantic?

A French social worker,
sipping Italian latte,
writes a report
on child labour.
The computer named after a fruit
she types on,
made by a 10-year-old Chinese girl
on 16-hour shifts
in a Taiwanese company.

They call it innovation.

A young Nepali cook,
working in a Goan restaurant
throws in red chilli peppers
that travelled with the Portuguese
from Mexico to India
on a 15th century journey
to make a famous pork vindaloo.

Do red chillies have existential crises?

'Two spoons sugar'
says the business-class passenger
as he grabs the butt cheeks of the stewardess,
while the flight passes over
Caribbean plantations.
Centuries of African slavery
mixed in tea, he drinks.

They call it heritage.

Tomahawk missiles,
America arrogantly names
weapons sent
to destroy Syria.
Centuries of indigenous culture,
The settlers still try to axe
'Burn, burn, burn'.

Do you hear the violence when they explode?

A Japanese school boy
still feels the terror of 9/11
but knows not about
schools bombed this morning
in Gaza.
Knows not about the
factory strike across his street.

They call it the power of global news.

A Russian gay man
who has never travelled
beyond his village,
watches a Wong Kar Wai film.
His tears in the shower
become the Iguazu falls.

Does loneliness have no borders?

A young subversive jailed
in a Montevideo prison
since 1981,
looks up to see
a patch of the sky,
the size of the blue handkerchief
his mother
pinned on his school uniform
when he was a little boy.

They call this the justice system.

A white feminist in the UN
is cheered on,
by the crowd,
yet again
drowning out
the voices of
valiant black women
and militant trans women

A feminism that belongs to all women?

But

the rap
in South Bronx then
becomes
angry Tamil rap
in the slums of Chennai now.

Vogueing by black latino queens
in ballrooms in Harlem
becomes
Vogueing on rooftops
in Thailand now.

The Black panthers
in 1966 Oakland,
become
The Dalit panthers
in 1972 Bombay.

A 60-year-old Hijra in Pakistan
Homeless in 1976,
becomes
Mother to a homeless 14-year-old
in 1993.

New skin stubbornly
Grows over old and new wounds.

Proud scars
That tell stories of tender love.

Azaadi
is still fought for
on the streets of Gaza,
the valley of Kashmir.

'We are still here'
Native American warriors,
draw murals
on university walls of colonisers.

Don Durito, the pipe smoking beetle
deep inside the Lacandon jungle,
still writes back to
10-year-old Mexican girls.

Bandit queens are born
in Dalit homes every day to make
many thousand years of caste patriarchy
beg on his knees for forgiveness.

An Iron Lady from Manipur
refuses food for 14 years
in protest against the cold brutality
of the Indian army.

Soft, curly black hair
on the chin

of the trans man writing this poem,
a triumphant beard at last!

We call this the resistance.

The resistance
Miriam Makeba
and
Nina Simone
still sing
from heaven above.

The revolution of our people.

Poly Love

His clit, slippery under my wet tongue
he grabs me close,
digging his bitten nails into my back
as I slip away
into memories of another love. Requited.
And fantasies of another. Unrequited.

Her curls tied into a bun,
loose strands flying carelessly, beckoning?
Smell of cigarettes and lust
become one.

I come.
Look at us,
making love with frenzied haste.

Slug sex, mid-air,
young lovers, too scared.

HOSHANG MERCHANT

Hoshang Merchant is the author of *Yaraana, Forbidden Sex/Texts, The Man Who Would be Queen* and *Sufiana*. His selected poetry is in *My Sunset Marriage*. He taught at Hyderabad University for twenty-six years. His four volume *Collected Poems* is published by Writers Workshop.

My Sister Takes a Long Long Time to Die

It was the dark of winter
When the illness came like a thunderclap
They isolated an Indian girl in the Chicago snow
Hoping this Indian disease would go away
But it was America that had killed her
The sickness in us is named America
And the long long time of waiting does not die

She had waited long in the dark of her lord
The lord she called father who never had a kind word
The lord who giveth and taketh away
(And now is the time of taking away)
The man she calls lord and manservant
The lover with fair hair and blue eyes
Who ferries her hither and thither like Charon

My sister, she hangs by our slender thread that cannot snap
Because the long long time of waiting is never dead

And she called Death as her brother
Brilliant, charismatic death
Death who loves and beguiles and kills
        but does not beget
Death the brother who no sister in life can wed
That unfulfilled love, that great longing that does not die
That long long time of waiting never dies

And now in the brilliance of summer
of melting light and butterflies
She floats between dark and light
As on a river a swan doubly glides
One half flesh; one half shadow
Sister and brother/Reality and reflection on one river

She has crossed life's flood on a reed
She awaits a boat now to ferry her to the other side
The long long wait she waits for all of us will never die...

Sind

'I have sinned' — Napier

It was with a Sindhi boy I first found love
He felt love but being a boy he took me from behind
Like the Holy Spirit took St John one night on the steep stairway
to god

It was a cold night
The train was tearing through the heart of Hindustan
And when it halted at a station
It was dawn and our love was known...

When the Indus meets the sea
It forgets it was the cold daughter of the snow
It becomes warm and shallow, lost in the sand
This land of sand
They call Sind

And the Arabs came
And finding Hindus there
They called this land of quicksands, Hindustan

The boys turned Turk soon enough
Eyes became mirrors for reflected lights of other gods
Warm love was pressed like wine between students and Master

People forgot their own names
They remembered the Name
Which too they soon forgot: Why do you ask the Name? They asked
And remembered only love

A cowherd played the pipe
A king followed him into the forest
A son of the Mughal on his way to conquer Kabul
Remembered to note the Hindu gods in Persian

And when times turned savage opium helped the heirs to die
painlessly
And Death turned a friend when a brother turned fiend
But to face death – without opium?
Or to face life – without poetry!

The river ran red that day
The women carried their breasts on a plate for the rapists
Men carried their heads in their hands for the conqueror

And poems that mention these ravages
Now gather dust at railway stations
But the milk of Sajal, the wine of Rumi
The breath of the breeze blown through a 'ney'
Say: He!

As I remember him in whose hands I died:
Thought stopped then like that night-train
And my heartbeat became a public event.

MINAL HAJRATWALA

Minal Hajratwala wrote *Leaving India: My Family's Journey from Five Villages to Five Continents* (winner of four nonfiction awards), *Bountiful Instructions for Enlightenment* (poetry), and the *Moon Fiji* travel guidebook (2019); edited *Out! Stories from the New Queer India* (anthology) and co-founded The (Great) Indian Poetry Collective.

Ghazal

22/1/95, San Francisco

Open your eyes, friend. Give up the green pretending.
Let's live only in the kaleidoscope of our communal dreams.

Three women sleep in a close circle, heads to feet.
sharing blankets all afternoon. Dissolving into dreams.

Don't you crave the salt-fat taste of sausage, brie, dark gumbo?
And the sweet-fat of desserts, the creamy pale of dreams?

The neon fish are guzzling, we can hear them
getting drunker every moment on bubbles and algae dreams.

The only truths left are the ones we create. No one is to blame.
The whole soul of Minal is in this inhaling, these last and lasting
    dreams.

Incantation for the Occasion

for Mala and Vega

The first step
is taken
in the heart – that trip,
that small sweet stumble
toward.

    The second step
    is surer,
    a gift to the stranger.
    A boot slides off and
    props open a door.

        The third step
        conjugates
        her pace, asks
        Whose path shall we walk
        today?

            As rivers
            surging
            don't weigh the rain
            who can count
            the fourth step?

The fifth step
might twist
a shin, meaning
There is always a choice,
so choose.

The sixth step
takes in
the world, remakes
the world with the logic
of two.

The seventh step
stretches
homeward, lifetimes,
ignites the true story –
the origin of flame.

FATIMAH ASGHAR

Fatimah Asghar is the author of the poetry collection *If They Come for Us* (2018) and the chapbook *After* (2015). She is also the writer and co-creator of the Emmy-nominated web series *Brown Girls*. In 2017, she was awarded the Ruth Lily and Dorothy Sargent Rosenberg Fellowship from the Poetry Foundation and was featured on the Forbes' 30 Under 30 list.

Pluto Shits on the Universe

On 7 February 1979, Pluto crossed over Neptune's orbit and became the eighth planet from the sun for twenty years. A study in 1988 determined that Pluto's path of orbit could never be accurately predicted. Labelled as 'chaotic', Pluto was later discredited from planet status in 2006.

Today, I broke your solar system. Oops.
My bad. Your graph said I was supposed
to make a nice little loop around the sun.

Naw.

I chaos like a motherfucker. Ain't no one can
chart me. All the other planets, they think

I'm annoying. They think I'm an escaped
moon, running free.

Fuck your moon. Fuck your solar system.
Fuck your time. Your year? Your year ain't
shit but a day to me. I could spend your
whole year turning the winds in my bed. Thinking
about rings and how Jupiter should just pussy
on up and marry me by now. Your day?

That's an asswipe. A sniffle. Your whole day
is barely the start of my sunset.

My name means hell, bitch. I am hell, bitch. All the cold
you have yet to feel. Chaos like a motherfucker.
And you tried to order me. Called me ninth.
Somewhere in the mess of graphs and math and compass
you tried to make me follow rules. Rules? Fuck your
rules. Neptune, that bitch slow. And I deserve all the sun
I can get, and all the blue-gold sky I want around me.

It is February 7th, 1979 and my skin is more
copper than any sky will ever be. More metal.
Neptune is bitch-sobbing in my rearview,
and I got my running shoes on and all this sky that's all mine.

Fuck your order. Fuck your time. I realigned the cosmos.
I chaosed all the hell you have yet to feel. Now all your kids
in the classrooms, they confused. All their clocks:
wrong. They don't even know what the fuck to do.

36

They gotta memorize new songs and shit. And the other planets, I fucked their orbits. I shook the sky. Chaos like a motherfucker.

It is February 7th, 1979. The sky is blue-gold: the freedom of possibility.

Today, I broke your solar system. Oops. My bad.

ANAHITA SARABHAI

Anahita is a queer performing artist, educator, poet and activist, currently based in Ahmedabad, Gujarat. She is also the founder-director of QueerAbad, Ahmedabad's only Queer-Ally community building initiative and online platform. Generally, she does far too much for her own good and can't seem to stop acquiring unexpected hats to wear.

W 164th St

You rest your head against my chest
hoping to hear more than the drumming
your breath falls into time with mine
as I wonder about the sound of the ocean
your arm encircles me and you pull yourself closer
hoping for more than waves against bone

you shift, once, twice, three times
and sigh, nuzzling into that nook
a place of comfort found between clavicle and breast
here you can feel the heat of my mouth,
hear my thoughtless humming as you wait.

On the sidewalk below a new hand of cards is dealt.

SRESHTHA

Sreshtha is a queer poet from Delhi and one of the founding editors of *The Shoreline Review*, an online journal for & by South Asian poets. She studied literatures in English from Delhi University & completed her MFA at Sarah Lawrence College. She currently lives & teaches in Las Vegas.

The Sonneteer Gets a Heartbreaker's Haircut

scalp clipped close to lose stray curls // she kept
nodding as he asked *shorter? now? how*
about this – shorter still? // needed the razor to graze
her as deep as any pivotal epiphany in some White Hollywood flick
Slick bangs to forehead stuck cigarette behind her ear
& practised smoulder on unsuspecting heterosexuals on the F train.

Every time her mother sobs *can't remember when you used*
to look pretty her breath breaks from all bones at once –
can you be ugly in intention? // at graduation, she trades
treasured tux for saree // her garb belongs to the women in her breasts:
blouse to Ma; silk to Grandma; spun gold to Calcutta

and though she is woman herself // will always be woman even with
    hat-stuffed hair,
in the pictures: her sweat-shined saree smiles in the sunlight bright
like mother's own she has never felt more // straightened more blatant
    more buoyant more boy

my high school nemesis finds me on instagram &
messages saying *oh shit S, you still like, a fucking lesbo?*

lesbo: like *let's go beat the shit out of that fucking lesbo*

like *listen bro I'm all about gay rights & shit but not you too*

like *they know what's coming for them if they so much as look at me so…*

like *aap jaise log toh ek number ke tharki hote ho*

like *just grow a pair you know you want to*

like *guess who*

like *spread & show us how much you want it then come on*

like fresh-boned slaughter still & slow

light against bleat-dressed goat

like *bitch blow you'll learn — wait what do you mean by you*

like *it so … hetero but not?*

like less is bore

like blessed ho be thy game

like *I know I only kissed you that one time & I never asked if it was okay
just went for it hard & hurried but I can't stop any more fuck I think
I'm, like a fucking lesbo who wants to fuck a lesbo, so you in or no?*

This Is Not Yet Another Poem About My Mother

C and I are navigating shower sex when I think

of my mother.

At 8, I kissed my first
    cigarette. Crouched under a bathroom sink, I sucked
                    the wrong end of a half
smoked *navy cut*, my palms stuck to the wall
                    in celebration or balance or both.

My mother walked in without knocking, crushed
        my coolness to ash and we never spoke about it again.

In another country, I am still afraid of my mother
                    walking in on knowledge she doesn't want.

Like how cigarette and woman come

together in the bedroom, the only warmth – my flame-licked

        skin, and her tensed tongue armed to tease them both.

Over the phone, my mother says: 'Everyone has father issues these
days. To be a successful poet, you should make up mother issues.'

Mothers are a black thread twisted around my shoulder
                    blades wrapped into stiffness.
C says love, says won't you meet
    my Mamma, says what does your mother look /

like? I say love me like a mother won't

I tell C no one loves me like a mother would.
       C says no one loves a fragile queer. I choke
                                on words sliced out

What I am trying to say is:
C slips on soap
      and my arms – maddening in its fumbles – become
                                my mother's

My shoulder shoved
                  against the chill of mirror reflects my mother's
My thirst tumbles
      down C's throat, burns
                      into the sound of my mother.

That yesterday, I went to this barbecue joint for dinner and I spent
                the entire time spying on our neighbour's order.

That sometimes, I laugh at my jokes for too long when no one else
does, & turn into my mother.

FIRAQ GORAKHPURI

Firaq Gorakhpuri (1896-1982), pen-name for Raghupati Sahay, was a
noted Urdu poet .In a 1936 essay, Firaq rebuked a contemporary critic
irked by boy-love in ghazals, by saying, 'are you aware of Socrates's
autobiography, and his relationship with Alcibiades ... Are you
aware of Shakespeare's sonnets ... Have you heard Sappho's name?'

Different from the world's secret

Different from the world's secret is the secret that I hide,
Different is that clever glance when it meets my eye.

Some Saviours are different from the fabled Jesus Christ.
Different is their magic touch, their heart, their style.

Enough was your memory to rob me of respite,
Should they also needle me, your lips, locks and eyes?

The knot of your coiling locks is difficult to untie,
Different are these knotted curls from the web of life.

Weeping, wailing can't produce music from the lyre of love,
Sorrow has a different tone, love has a different style.

All of us are pushing ahead towards the bounds of world beyond.
And the voice of bygone days pulls us back, besides.

The beauteous eye continues to feed the flame of life,
While your lovers are engaged in a life and death strife.

Translated from the Urdu by K.C. Kanda

KARUNA CHANDRASHEKAR

Karuna is a queer feminist writer from India. Her work has been published online and in print. Though she wishes otherwise, love, loss and language remain the broad concerns of her poems.

aftermath

Every time she leaves
I break hourglasses / I refuse the gift of regret.
When she returns
with her hands empty / and eye bruised / like a child's knees
I whisper / forget your emptiness
you are the night's husk.

I have uttered her name / like falling lilies /from a clenched fist / at a
gravesite
her name / is the last wishbone / to fill the china of my palm / its
madness
echo / I have read like psalms.

She pretends she has not heard
the jacarandas chatter / how I have been livid with love
viscous with blood / a heavy duty wire sparking / in a vicious flood.

Her heart's incoherence / is a fist full of flowers
stuffed in the raw mouth of childhood /
she refuses the gift of deliverance /
and I am the bruised fruit / of this resistance.

Every morning / she blinds each eye
to love me,
every night / I sleep dreamless
a wolf cut from her howl.

 I have watched dreams die / ships sinking
in a sea's wail / a neon stoplight / blinking its last /
on a deserted highway.

Yet I am still wild / teeth and hair / dust and bones /
a hurricane's eye open wide, wild /
so there.

Translation / Delhi: a love story

like a boat trapped on land / I see the sea / a mirage at the end of
every gully / this city is a pit of fire / and I am an ant crossing a
wire / over its flames / I think I might love or die over here / I learn
to do both and neither.

sitting cross-legged in a gurdwara / you say, 'close your eyes and hear
god speak'/ a pool reflects the night / stars meet our bare feet / fish
dart across the sky / waiting / but nothing / on a rickshaw ride
home / your knee touches mine / 'god's whisper'.

dust haunts all my belongings / the sky is the back end of an oven
/ my back baking like bread / this city only hungers for itself / so
rename each heart / 'thirst' / and be done with it / if I am the arrow /
then my target has left / the heat is bitter / but I am still more

dance as if possessed / in the crush of bodies / in the unceasing
music of wind / in a song as foreign as a lover's tongue / 7 believers
take flight into *peshi* / 7 pagodas rise within me / fingers of light
trace the lattice / I am still learning to live with myself / to dance and
possess.

these days / I happen somewhere / where I am not / the distance
between home and here / is 2168 kilometers / but I have forgotten /
the smell of salt / I have forgotten / I was marooned once / I
have learned to respond to the word *mehfil*/ / like I do to a bird call /
riding the waves, / my body becomes the sound.

AQDAS AFTAB

Aqdas Aftab is a non-binary writer, reader and dreamer from Islamabad, currently getting their PhD in trans of colour literature at the University of Maryland. Aqdas is often thinking about queer speculation, prison abolition and the healing power of dandelions. Their words can be found in *Bitch Media*, *The Rumpus*, *Kajal Magazine*, *Yes Poetry* and the anthology *Transcendent 4: The Year's Best Speculative Transgender Fiction*.

All Death

Teach your students trans petals and poetics, just not all death.

Critiqcritiqcritique rac-ing states, but you too, sought all death.

Pretend you breathe life into humans by reading afresh big books –

Oh c'mon now – a shift in hermeneutics never fought all death!

God rolled her eyes at liberals so hard, Her gaze got stuck in firdaus,

White professors still strut silly, even after their pens begot all death.

A friend texts another suicide attempt, another tectonic plate splits.

Weeping in panic, Azraeel promises, he did not plot all death.

Exhausted, you beg her, 'tear open my scalp, lick my bleeding brain'
The tools are ready. 'No, use your nails.' In bed you forgot all death.

Tonight you want hard choking, her curls coiled around your neck,
Sweet way to lose breath. Maybe her tenderness will cumblot all death.

JOSHUA MUYIWA

Joshua Muyiwa is a poet, writer and columnist, not yet thirty-four, he started writing because he was told, 'it is time to stop seeming arty and pretentious and actually earn the tags by doing something'. He is queer. He lives in Bangalore.

Mouth

Imagine, we could go back.
Back in time, to when to truly know something,
we had to put it in our mouths.
Your mouth is late February. It is a cherry.
Sweet on first nip. And then only gets sweeter till drifting is
inevitable.
Your mouth is sometimes December. Bitter winter.
The kind of winter that East European men will declare mild while
you are shivering.
Your mouth is sometimes uninviting.
Unlike these men, who were willing to taste everything once.
My sweat. Charms. Lots of hash from Morocco.
The hot chilli sauce from Wok & Go.
And beer in every form.
      Imagine, we could go back.

The warning that everything on the Redcoat Isle is inedible and
tasteless,
holds true for everything (and everyone) that is not exported or
holidaying.
Though, I realised I had come back home on tasting
my grandmother's ground chilli chutney.
The mouth is the library.
My first lover: he tasted of Cinthol behind the ears.
And like Axe Body Spray near his armpits and pubes.
My grandmother's chutneys are always generous on chilli.
My grandfather's food on the garlic.
My best friend puts generous amounts of tomato in all his food.
My flatmate likes lime. But all this, you already know.
Your mouth on the other hand isn't so excited by spice,
not interested in the juicy, the overwhelming, the fleshy, the violent.
So much these orifices register.
So much your orifices register.
So much my orifices register.

Knees

Capped, conquering and careful – your knee.

Such concern, so crystalline.

Nothing tougher, nothing bolder.

It can also bend.

In bed, your knees have found my warmth, lingered and pushed –

only to meet resistance, restraint and refrain:

equal parts yielding to being desired, equal parts fearing sweet,
   crushing death.

You've always been so gentle with your tools.

Tougher, bolder at times.

Like a rabbit boring its way through the downs.

Your knees have purpose, they've got principles and are quite the
   pervert.

Your knees always betray your mind with a knock –

under the table of a dingy bar, they've been bumped into me to
   remind me

that I'm here with you,

and no one else, not even my own self,

on sofas at dinner parties, they've egged me on to speed up my good-
   byes,

at nightclubs and over nightcaps, it tallies my cigarettes

and chides me on my excesses,

digging into the small of my back in the middle of the night,

they prompt me to dissolve into you.

You know, one of my lovers would always invite

me to things with the question:

Would you like to join?

I love this awkward phrasing. It glows with possibility.

It made me feel like on encountering each other,
we'd immediately lose all boundaries
and merge into the other. (He always disappointed.)
Your knees remind me
that at night turning into putty on your knob ensures
in the morning, we'll be pliable,
plastic and pleased.

RUSHATI MUKHERJEE

Rushati Mukherjee is a journalist, blogger, translator and poet who identifies as 'ambisexual', mirroring the ambiguity she experiences about her sexuality. Her writings on sexuality and trauma have been published in *Feminism in India*. Her poems have been published in *The Bangalore Literary Review* and *Berlin Art-Parasites*.

Shots

lick the smoke that
     curls out
from your languid
     mouth
      unceasingly.
run my tongue
     through the
        outline of your winging
     ribs
bone-struck.
scratch the pure white flesh
     s t r e t c h e d
 unarmed under your skin

     sunk in.

trace the   of your navel,
      dip
       concave,
disappearing, and imagine
     lower in.
     blow the powder into the air
and watch it swirl
     like pixie dust
eyes bloom
     like flakes of rust
smoke swirls
like g
     a
        r
          l
        a
     n
   d
s of grass

 tartn-
ess s-
lide-
s dow-
n t-
he si-
de o-
f the g-
lass

                lipstick-stained,
                orgasm-bubbled
cigarettes
                unfurl maddeningly
twilight
                falls
fairylights twinkle
desiringly
 seductively
touch your arms
 and breathe in time
 utterly
 repeatedly
s \ l \ i \ c \ e \ m \ y \ m \ i \ n \ d \ i \ n \ t \ o \ p \ i \ e \ c \ e \ s
a n d w a n d e r t h r o u g h r e a l
i t y
//hyper-
                //hyper-
                        //seizurely
leisurely
leisurely

KAZIM ALI

Kazim Ali was born in the UK of Indian parents. His books include poetry, essay, and fiction. *All One's Blue: New and Selected Poems* was released in India by HarperCollins. He is a professor of transnational literature at the University of California, San Diego.

Divination

Square and circle my birth chart impresses

Drawn to separate a single clear note emerging

From a wash of ambient sound of stars and planets

Individual notes discrete revolve around the sun

Here I am a threaded bead impaled by decades

By prayers I can't see or hear but slide along the thread

Neither the one praying nor the prayer itself

Just a clot of muscle and bone counting

I spin how clouds condense amber from the tree

Driftwood on the Baltic smooth under the palm

All roughness eroded on a map of the mountain's ridges

In color liken themselves to some other place

Algeria rhymes with Paraguay or Taiwan and Morocco with Chile or
   Bhutan

Confusion and utterance

South wind southern

Shuttered shut torn as per usual

Devil and his split tongue gives a word as another word

In the Generalife of the Alhambra we saw an Arab couple with their
   lonely planet guide

And the cypress tree leaning over

It may have witnessed the assignation but it looks dead to me

How much we want to hold on to history

I want to hold in my arms

My many lives

The one when I flew with blue wings

Or when I was on my back covered in sculptor's dust

Or when I spied the Arab couple with a guide book in Hebrew

Or the time in the grey city I wanted to strangle myself

With flowers and mist stoking infernos in my rib cage

Reading the *Master Letters* in the coffee shop of the bus station

Solid cold sky wet on my skin

My chest a prisoned cathedral

Never told in the park the winter brought

I am forgotten how to draw myself

In ice on the glass that no one told shattered

Chapters of tinsel dark lust and angry loneliness

I disappeared then amidst thrum and hunger

If you want to know the edge of ocean or sky

Water and air unloosens itself

Pitched into the season of orange

No weapon but green

I lost myself in the sedimented time of petrified woods

You are a door leading nowhere in the slopes of ardor and crime

Heretics used to burn

Your heresy is you believe the body has a mind and a spirit too

That it is a ladder to god

That bones and muscle are

Bricks of Babel

Of course you could try to actually look at yourself

Lie and say so casually oh it just came to me in the rain

I put a jacket of mist and flowers in my suitcase

All the contracts of lethargy and forgetfulness

I've refused to sign and on the other side of the glass

A friend I don't recognize, the brave one

Who unpacked all my shirts of silence

And now who am I without them

When I open my mouth

There's nothing left inside

I am only myself to throw now, grown into bell and ghost garden bird

Third every night to soar

Petals in my mouth

I want a big pocketful of coins now

Cents crazy you will be and festooned

Yes I is you

The papers are all writing stories about you

It's the now that will be your lover

Stripped in summer suck

Stringed to the sky wingless

You will be a knot of cleverness

This crime is my second offense

Accordion to conventional wisdom

The wind that carries the siren-song landwards

A land word land bridge my second or third try

Ken you quickly tell me

Ken you quickly kell me

When I thought up logos I foundered

Old ghost caused almost

There built I in the roots of the earth

A stone laboratory my labor labial

Pronounce a nonce announce

I can't spell your sin

Spill to the rest

To the west the third most important shrine

To color always counting god by shade

This flower book dehisces not close to you

Feeling in wonder through

The powder of gold air flouring

Fleet that sluices through

You sailed yourself to the end of vision

You spent are spent passed hand in hand

Lust spawn sent in throes of flower

Now petal yourself astronomical

Sky flower throw your voice of light

Petal yourself labialalluvial

Soaked clear through luminous spent

Kneeling before intensity why should the vessel be always unscathed

Why should the I always be spared

Don't you want to know you have been passed through

Exit Strategy

I hear the sound of the sprinkler outside, not the soft kind we used
to run through but the hard kind that whips in one direction then
cranks back and starts again.

Last night we planned to find the white argument of the Milky Way
but we are twenty years too late. Last night I cut the last stargazer
lily to wear in my hair.

This morning, the hardest geography quiz I've ever taken: how does
one carry oneself from mountain to lake to desert without leaving
anything behind?

Perhaps I ought to have worked harder.
Perhaps I could have paid more attention.
A mountain I didn't climb. Music I yearned for but could not achieve.

I travel without maps, free-style my scripture, pretend the sky is an
adequate representation of my spiritual beliefs.

The sprinkler switches off. The grass will be wet.
I haven't even gotten to page 2 of my life and I'm probably more than
halfway through, who knows what kind of creature I will become.

UNITY YAMAZAKI

Unity Yamazaki is a queer Fijian-Indian woman from Aotearoa New Zealand living on Gadigal land in Australia. She writes about racism, oppression and broken love with hope and dark humour. She has featured at events in Sydney and Delhi, and has had two poems shortlisted for the *Overland* Fair Australia Prize.

kindergarten

kissing a white girl, a close second to being one
in my imaginary world, I had both

sweet dripping oranges lead to sticky fingers lead to sand
pit dramas lead to art corner
nerves

the other kids
keep a safe distance stealing
glances they can justify as a whole number away
from staring
like their parents had taught them

I stood
paintbrush in hand

all the colours of the rainbow
close at heart
rebuilding the immigrant dream
one muddy artwork at a time

struggling to articulate
what I knew
what I knew not to say

CHITHIRA VIJAYAKUMAR

Chithira Vijayakumar is a genderqueer journalist and poet who works on issues of land, technology, gender, and decolonization. They also work with theatre as a medium for addressing oppression and trauma. They are currently working on a book about the Periyar river in Kerala.

33 Worlds

My brilliant lover, as a gift, gives me a slideshow. Now I know what you're thinking, but wait, hear me out here.

She prints out minuscule photographs of our moments together, three for every month we've been together – so that's 99. When I say minuscule, I mean the size of crushed salt, or a star ... you could fit thousands on a single postage stamp.

But they're not so small that you can't see them; each photograph is a discrete shape in my palm.

One by one, she lays them face-down onto my open eyes. Then she holds my hand. I blink once, twice, and then in an incandescent flurry, the photos come into focus.
I'm watching a film in the planetarium of my eyelids.

I simply have to move my eyes from left to right, and back again, to scroll through the photos. I go through them one by one, then I go back and forth, and then I swish smoothly through them all. There's this intimate squeeze within my skull, a grip of love.

Suddenly, I'm beginning to understand why love is a terrifying thing. She loves me, and wants me to know it. She could crush me like a bug. And I would go happily, dead and smiling in the sunlight.

On an Afternoon Spent Gently Unhooking Stars
Caught in Barbed Wire

a home is an easy thing to lose
like safety pins, bookmarks, or minds.
sometimes you leave it behind on a park bench and board a bus
and by the time you've made your way back, it's gone,
pocketed by someone who needed it more.

sometimes a home collapses around you like rain,
and now nothing remains in the space
between you and the stars.
sometimes the tree you planted in your childhood garden
splits the brick wall in half,
and the axes come out of the woodshed,
blinking in the sudden light of day.

at other times, you simply wake up and find
that you'd gone to sleep somewhere else, elsewhere
in another body;
and you are a stranger here
to them, to yourself.

some homes look like deceit,
turn into mirrors,
into mines,
into sunken boats,
into teeth,
into train tickets,
into ballot boxes.

tonight, the wind is knives.
how do you know when you've loved someone enough –
enough to turn them into a home?
into a place you move into, with nothing in hand, no clothes on your
back.

bathe me,
feed me,
shroud me in an old blanket
and then we'll stand on the stoop,
the border grazing our feet,
barbed wire pressing softly against our soles.

OROOJ-E-ZAFAR

Orooj-e-Zafar is a genderqueer poet moonlighting as a doctor in their hometown: Islamabad, Pakistan. Orooj is the author of two poetry collections, *heart the size of a loosening fist* and *Home & Other Debris*. They are also Pakistan's National Slam Champion 2018, a two-time TEDx speaker, a comedian for the Auratnaak Movement and conduct storytelling workshops at lower primary, middle and high schools.

My Sister, by Land

I taste sea-salt at your mention, friend
as if your name runs deeper than the sensitivity of coral,
as if the ocean exhumed you for causing it insecurity –
friend, your depth is a wonder the earth has not seen yet.

You utter, 'lovebug', in a shade of comfort I cannot help
but force the black on my back into perfect concentric spots,
burning in my red. Friend, I would topple the horizon
just to tattoo your upper lip with the Big Dipper.

Afghanistan bled right into my city –
it excised parts of my heart before I knew your smile.

You are the reason Pakistan will ever know it was kind,
you were always running towards me.

Friend, I don't envy the blind around you. I only wish
your heart bleeds gold right into their good intentions;
I can only hope that your skin, dyed congenitally
with anger and too much strength, does not sink
into your own bones. I pray for the day, heaven breaks its gates
just to ask you how you have managed to grace the earth
before its time.

I don't know if you've ever swum an ocean at night, but I know,
when you live vicariously through me you see the purple winking
in the skyline, past the two dots tucked behind the moon –
crazed into oblivion till dawn. You are my point A, friend;

when the world cannot walk the white line
and laughs for being tipsy, I want to know we were buried in the
debris together so even in the end, when hope feels a lot like
suffocating
under the same earth too scared to spit us back home,

you know that your hand is not one I'm letting up,
your glow isn't one to lose its lustre with abuse,
your eyes tell more stories than all the ears in the world can hold.

I hope you know, friend,
heaven could not help but crack open its soil
to search for the white we could only find
in your eyes.

SMITA V.

Smita V. is a queer feminist who works on gender, sexuality, and technology. They are interested in stories, books, history, tech, fandoms, art, and in queering all of it. She can be generally found wandering the cyberspace or on a hunt for good coffee.

People say 'I love you' all the time.

'Hey, all okay?'

'Text me when you reach.'

'Want me to make you some coffee?'

'Imbecile.'

'Why haven't you eaten yet?!'

'I heard this song, and thought you'd like it.'

'Here, I got you some fries.'

'Get up. I made you breakfast.'

'Hurry up!' *pause* 'Please don't run.'

'I want you to have this book.'

'Of course you should get that Star Wars t-shirt! And that Doctor Who one too.'

'I think you need this (good) whiskey more than me.'

'Dinner kiya?'

'Weirdo.'

climbs four floors

'Your food is getting cold.'
'Please tell me you have a scarf?'
'Yeh lo, bread aur cheese.'
'Call?'
'Pagal.'
'I'll wait for you.'
'Jackass.'
'Hugs.'
'Have you packed your underwear?'

People say 'I love you' all the time.

ALISHYA ALMEIDA

Alishya Almeida has spent her life in Bahrain and India in an almost equal measure of years. She was a teaching fellow at Ashoka University for courses in literature, gender studies, art, and film studies. She is now pursuing her graduate studies at Lehigh University in the United States.

Treating oneself to a honey moon

Two women scoff at each other in moonlight
blue. I'm here searching for a dancing river.
I am no poet at home. It's a gift to do that.
Some tales leave the order in order to be written,
stirring sideways a boat through the tendrils of war
to find themselves. I know both the women
but fill my cup without them. I am alone here.
Two make a pair, but love is between
two halves that aren't about fitting.
Instead, filling out space
because the other can take it.
Is the queer built to arrive at sex?
The way in museums I am the safest

under a scene of sex because everyone

has it locked in closets, clothed in impressions.

I do not know other methods

for anger but only as the silence I elongate

in cities that have no history of my mistakes yet.

I continue by melting the past in my coffee,

fumble in languages not mine

and rewarded with forgiveness:

lick my wounds please.

I even brought an umbrella

but this rain won't sigh here, teasing.

All these people aware, unaware

of this waiting for the rain but

I want the guzzle of pouring to eat me.

I always meet the sorrow in a person first.

These two women too ache in voluminous want.

What might that tell you about a condition

in which one loves crumbly cake left after spoonfuls,

and the paint when falling off their faces?

I must not tidy before I pause to leave here

only varnish before I leave the pause here.

SHAKTI MILAN SHARMA

Shakti Milan Sharma does a lot! At the same time, he feels like he does nothing. Sometimes he gets tired with the burden of layers which get attached to his identity. He wants you to sketch his bio from your imagination & if you can't, that's fine too.

लागा jockey में दाग

लागा jockey में दाग, छुपाऊं कैसे?

cab is unavailable, घर जाउं कैसे?

jockey का दाग धुलाऊं कैसे?

घर जाउं कैसे?

भूल गया सब वचन पिता के

खो गया मैं PR/Grindr पे आके

जाके भाई को quickie का मतलब समझाउं कैसे?

घर जाउं कैसे?

कोरी jockey soul मोरी

Douche है माया जाल

ये दुनिया मेरी fetishes का घर

वो दुनिया boredom का hall
जाके मम्मी से नज़रें मिलाऊं कैसे?
घर जाउं कैसे?
लागा jockey में दाग, छुपाऊं कैसे?
cab is still unavailable, घर जाउं कैसे?

Poet's note: This poem is a response to the song *'Laaga Chunari Mein Daag',* sung
by Manna Dey.

SNEHA KHAUND

Sneha Khaund is a doctoral researcher at Rutgers University. She was a Commonwealth Scholar at the Centre for Cultural, Literary and Postcolonial Studies at SOAS and has worked in publishing in New Delhi.

Testing limits

Take a moment
Stretch it like gum
Wrap it over your back
Pull your arms across your stomach
Spread them out to see how far you extend.

Testing limits II

I push at the air
Touching my arms
Plastered to me like sticky rice
I withdraw
Shrink
Swim like a man with horn-rimmed glasses
In the jelly of my freedom
I push my arms outwards
Attempting to be a waterproof butterfly
I press my eyes shut
Shut closed
A kaleidoscope bursts
As the air touches
Makes me again.

IFTIKHAR NASIM

Iftikhar Nasim (1946–2011), better known to his friends and readers as Ifti, wrote in Urdu and English. He is the first modern openly gay Urdu poet from Pakistan. Nasim moved to Chicago in 1971. He is remembered for his books *Narman*, *Myrmecophile* and *Abdoz*, and for his activism.

Somrita Urni Ganguly is a professor, poet and literary translator. She translates from Bengali and Hindi to English. She has been published by Juggernaut Books, BEE Books, Seagull Books, and Hawakal Publishers; and in *Asymptote*, *Words Without Borders*, *In Other Words* and *Muse India*, among others.

My Father

Father,
Everyone says I look like you.
My eyes, my forehead, my lips,
My tone, the way in which I talk,
The way in which I walk,
The way I sit, the way I behave,
The way my lips quiver –
All my ways are yours.
It is said that a son is the true successor

Of his father's blood and race.
I therefore often ask myself,
If I am like you in every other way,
Why are my sexual desires
So different from yours?

Translated from the Urdu by Somrita Urni Ganguly

Translator's note: This work is for my friends and Ifti's, for accepting our quirks: Ajmal Kamal-ji, Mohtarma Neelum Ahmed Bashir, Nayyer Hayat Qasmi Sa'ab, and Prof. C.M. Naim.

NIKITA DESHPANDE

Nikita Deshpande is the author of *It Must've Been Something He Wrote*. Her work features in anthologies like *Magical Women* and *Grandpa Tales*, as well as *Buzzfeed*, *The Rumpus*, *Scroll* and *Grazia*, among others. She lives in Mumbai, where she competes with her partner to make the better cup of kaapi.

corrigendum

it was a long time ago
and I always picture rain
though mid-december
was upon us
with its expense
and promise of cheap pleasure.
(perhaps it is the fog
stretching itself
artfully
over the short time we had)

I'd grown up
swallowing Yash Chopra movies and
Mani Ratnam romances,
waiting

with my whole body
for a man's hand to tug me
gently
onto the footboard
of a moving train, driving
into a blazing forever

yet, here I was,
my heart beating
in a different part,
in the dark shadows
of the corridor
outside your house
where
among old leather shoes
and a bubbling fish tank
you held my face to yours
and taught me how to kiss.

we were nineteen
and foolish
and too obsessed with boys
to know.

such a long time ago.

will you forgive me
for the winding logic
and for thinking,
when like a bloodhound

I should have followed my nose
into the crook of your neck?

boys were so exciting.
they seemed like circus nets
for two girls walking
a tightrope
between them
and in the end, you jumped off
but I looked down first.

forgive me.
it was a long time after
I discovered how tongue tasted
like sea squid
and flesh like salt,
that I learned –
bodies are not puzzle pieces
but candle wax.

DHIREN BORISA

Dhiren Borisa is a poet and social geographer based in Delhi. In 2018, he finished his PhD on queer urban cartographies on gay male desires in Delhi at JNU. He writes in English, Hindi, Urdu and Gujarati. He recently finished his Visiting Fellowship at the University of Leicester.

Should I mourn a little longer?
after Rohith Vemula

Should I mourn a little longer

how he nursed a broken dream

how much
he nursed a broken dream

should I touch his night with words

should my lament
be stronger

how those who craved
autumn's last night

were exiled by the spring

how those in spring's light arms
were auctioned off as
autumn's claim

should I say his name
should I say each of their names

would you care to note them down
should your ink be darker
your hand, stronger

should I mourn
a little longer

the shrouds are again
leaving my part of the town

my town has again
erupted in flames

you will have to listen
to the screams of my people

you will have to listen to their names
you will have to keep count

the minister's recommendations
lie soaked in blood

stillborn
on the pages
of the Constitution

should I just close the file
junk the folder

should I ask the Harijans
to carry it on their shoulder

as you stand, mute
should I ask the Bahujans
to lend their hand

your silence has always been
a warmonger

should I mourn a little
longer

Translated from the Hindi by Akhil Katyal

TRISHNA SENAPATY

Trishna Senapaty is a queer poet and anthropologist from Delhi. She was short listed for the TFA award for creative writing in 2016. She is currently working on her PhD and is based in Ithaca, New York.

Crumbs

So much we've ever felt
is in the kitchen
between the cracking of egg shells
against greasy surfaces
and the thousand crumbs of burnt toast
on your shirt

You move noisily
from toaster to pan
back to refrigerator
I stir silently, dreamily
engrossed in the battering of shapes

You speak to your self
sometimes to me
I forgive that you steal my morning newspaper
before inviting me in for tea

You don't mind
I'm only pretending to help

I feed the cat
stretched on the ledge above your head

Between us we have
no hobbies, no people, no work
no secrets, no enemies

But for the warmth of cooking fire
and chance music drifting in
through the broken window
in the corner, what have we?

I gave you timelessness
You taught me the unpredictability
of green chillies.

RIDDHI DASTIDAR

Riddhi Dastidar is a non-binary/femme disabled poet and journalist in New Delhi. She is a postgraduate student of Gender Studies at Ambedkar University Delhi where she studies 'madness'. Her writing has been shortlisted for the TFA Award in 2019 and 2020, and the Himal Short Story Prize 2019. Her work has appeared or is forthcoming in *Rattle, Glass, Himal Southasian, Scroll.in, The Wire* and elsewhere.

Queer As In

Queer as in fuck you,
queer as in secret.
Queer as in just a phase, as in the very best of friends
arms interlinked with yours, smilingly saying
you just think it makes you interesting.

Queer as in only at parties, as in only when drunk,
as in only that one time at that party when drunk –
she has a boyfriend in real life, you know.
You know, queer as in not in real life.

Queer as in not really, no.
Queer as in crying at YouTube videos of white lesbians surprise-
proposing.
Josh Groban sings as Ellen and Portia never age, never fight
and Melissa Etheridge is The Only One. As in turn off the TV
when D.E.B.S is on and Lucy Diamond gets the girl.

Queer as in can only get off when thinking of women –
but everyone does that! Queer as in put your hands together
and beg forgiveness for putting your hands together
and getting off when thinking of women.

Queer as in 'with a girl?' about a date, on the phone with your mum.
As in how can you hurt us like this?
As in marriage is the Difficult Question you're skipping
to go look for those you can at least attempt to answer.
As in grandchildren won't fill the frame.

Queer as in spend childhood summers fighting, flicking
light-switch-on, light-switch-off – it's a panic-party!
Until the thought goes away tomorrow. Magical infinite tomorrows:
I will be a good girl tomorrow, I will not like girls tomorrow,
I will not talk to myself tomorrow. I will talk to my family
without crying tomorrow.

Tomorrow I'll come with you to Dokkhinneshwar, Ma,
but it's going to take more than flowers-prayers-proshaad because
I am never going to be any less abnormal, Ma,
sorry I couldn't be more normal, Ma.

Queer as in reddest lips and no hair, no lashes,
no lojja or labonnyo. No romanticising privacy
or boys taking me home to their mother
while Everyone Else We Know's daughters marry, Ma.

Queer as in how do I identify?
Not straight, not gay, not girl enough,
miles away from man. Just queer, man,
as in queer.
I dentif i
as queer.
I like the way it sounds like the start
of 'weird'. The way I don't have a plan.
Queer.

ZULFIKAR ALI BHUTTO

Zulfikar Ali Bhutto is a visual and performance artist, and curator of mixed Pakistani, Lebanese and Iranian descent. Bhutto's work explores complex histories of colonialism that are exacerbated by contemporary international politics. He unpacks the intersections of queerness and Islam through a multi-media art practice.

The New Leader

I've heard
He likes cats and dogs,
that means he must have a kind heart.

When she smiles it feels oh so genuine.

They have a good relationship with India,
an upside to this may mean we'll have peace.

They have a military background, so does that mean war?
in which case, we need to raise the walls of our house,
put in a reinforced gate,
make sure our passports are up to date,
renew our visas.

Oh but you can't do that anymore
so get new visas.

He's quite strict,
which is bad for some,
bad for the bad guys.
He'll lock 'em real quick.
harsher punishments mean less crime.

Bullshit.

Our drawing rooms need to become meeting spaces,
if not our drawing rooms,
our bedrooms,
if not our bedrooms then those dingy alley ways you meet your lovers
in for a quick blowjob and cock up the ass,
Hill park, Fraire Hall Gardens, that empty spot on Clifton beach,
you name it jaanu.

Take your non-verbal cruising, give it words, make it resistance,
make every conversation into an insinuation of revolution,
every wink, a portal into a new world order.

LEAH PIEPZNA-SAMARASINHA

Leah Lakshmi Piepzna-Samarasinha is a queer disabled non-binary femme writer of Burgher/Tamil Sri Lankan and Irish Roma ascent. The author of *Tonguebreaker, Care Work, Dirty River, Bodymap, Love Cake, Consensual Genocide* and co-editor of *The Revolution Starts At Home*, her work has won the Lambda and been short listed for the Publishing Triangle and Pushcart Awards.

My Father, Christmas 1991, As I Come Down the Stairs in Ripped Jeans and That Jane's Addiction T-Shirt with All the Naked People on It

a persona poem, for my beautiful, complicated, queer Sri Lankan dad. Thank you for making me who I am.

I am tense
I want her to take off those ripped jeans, that obscene t-shirt and put
    on something else.
It's Christmas
and this is not what I wanted for my life
this little wrenlike woman I am married to, this angular glaring
    daughter one shade lighter than me,
who hates me in her terrible green hair.

I want a drink.
I want to be alone in the basement,
with my heavy tumbler of Johnnie Walker Red, the history channel
   on low
something educational about Winston Churchill
some nice white man from the country that was the last place I felt
   alive and happy
which was twenty years ago
the dull humid cool of the beige wall to wall from the factory outlet,
   the old brown and orange nylon
plaid couch, my Heavy Metal comic books and a bar painted thick
   brown
that nobody uses but me

I do not want to be near my parents either.
I do not want to think about them, or write them back
to their thin blue aerogram letters from Australia
or pick up the phone when they call
in the tiny window between our time zones and half a world away
   where we are both awake
I don't want to think about my desire,
or how I tell the neighbors I am Portuguese,
or how far away I am from everything I knew
I lock it all in a box, my gender, my history, my parents,
all the islands I grew up on,
to live in this vinyl siding house surrounded by people I hate,
snow I hate
everything I hate but beer, TV, and silence

It's easy enough to put one foot in front of another
through my days

of paycheck, and then no paycheck, and fuming twisting barking
    orders
at this wife who works two jobs when I can't find any
and puts a line of pillows down the middle of the bed so we never
    touch
but I sleep in the basement so I can masturbate in peace, and sleep
    my five hours
and wake up to take the commuter train to someplace
that is at least a city, at least civilized
with coffee, and men I can look at in the bathroom of Filene's
    Basement on my lunch break

but there she comes, this angry brown daughter
who looks sort of like me, except she despises me
for how I drive the car too fast, shout her down for all her smart-ass
    remarks.
I don't know if she knows I learned to drive
the week before her mother gave birth to her
there were always trishaws, busses and the London Underground
    where I grew up.
I try to talk to her in the car as she turns up the volume of her yellow
    Walkman
so loud she can't even hear my voice

I know one day soon, as soon as she is done getting through college,
the way I couldn't, she is going to go to another country
with a big bag of clothes and a notebook, just like I did,
and not take our calls, answer our letters
She will go one step further and change her phone number, unlist it
    from the book,

change her name to some thing she says is both of ours she found
    researching her senior thesis,
which I could've told her
if she just asked.

I think she will like women,
or like tender leaning boys who I would've liked to like too
 like the one with his ringlets who shows up at the house with a hash
    brownie and roses for her.
My daughter is going to leave me here, with this silence, johnnie
    walker red, the history channel
the wren like woman getting quieter and quieter
my daughter is going to write a letter saying things I never dared to
    send to my parents
and close the door of the basement
gently,
firmly
in my face.

Parliaments on the stoop

For Fatima, after Orlando

There's nothing like being two kinds of sore-hipped brown femmes
a week after a hate crime,
smoking Parliaments on the stoop
outside a queer Black femme birthday party
with lots of glitter house looks.
It's safe to be inside, soft,
but we come outside
to be bad brown femmes looking at the moon
smoking in the bushes like we've trained for at every wedding.
We're watching the Islamophobia meter go up,
tracing frequencies of hair pat downs and panic attacks,
saying, *it feels just like after 9/11, girl,*
saying, *I think the government paid him to do that shit, he ain't ISIL.*
He's probably some closeted gay cousin whose an asshole to his wife
like we've known plenty of in our lifetimes.
The queer Muslim healing gathering was in the basement of an
   inaccessible bar,
we left after five minutes.
Bad brown girls always cluster in a bush
sucking fire and blowing smoke at the moon,
at what we never know how to survive
but sometimes don't
sometimes, do.

VIMAL BHAI

Vimal Bhai is a Gandhian environmental and social human rights activist, working in Uttarakhand in the Ganga & Yamuna Valley. He has written eighteen books on dam-related issues. He sculpts, paints and writes poetry. He believes in Nature because it never discriminates against anyone.

Rest

On your soft lips
a hint of a moustache,
    the cuts on your chest
    just visible
    inside your shirt
        and the inebriating rocks
        of your thighs

I have seen you from all sides –
    you are beautiful.

Come near me,
    I want to hold you
    captive, draw a line around you
        with the salt of my desire.

With an impatient kiss
　　　on your neck, let me give rest
　　　to all my years.

My history dissolved in heat.

Listen love
　　　how will we ever meet?

Translated from the Hindi by Akhil Katyal

VQUEERAM ADITYA SAHAI

Vqueeram lives and loves in Delhi.

sometimes i wish for a heterosexual romance

so i look very carefully
for that special everyday kinda man

in university corridors
a hegelian-but-not-marxist guy
to eventually get bored
of the endless addas and cups
after cups of pheeki chai

turn up early to a rock concert
to find the absolute opposite
throw a fit, break a few dishes
'coz he smells of the lead guitarist

or the tattooed dude
in the fifth row, the same day
who will too often, and for far too long, brood
when i lick his only bit of uninked nape

perhaps, an economics major with a decent job
in the striped shirt and the striped tie
who can't understand
why almadovar is crazy, why plath makes me cry

that hunkameat early morning jogger
makes even my imagination run, naked
he's a good fuck in those vacant plots but the raw
eggs in the morning and gym selfies would break it

at the diner, who waited on me with a dimpled smile
flirted as i took another cosmopolitan
dreams less of us and more of the child
he will spoil while i am in the kitchen

so go to bihar or eastern UP
to find the bollywood lover
who sings guru dutt,
a break from colour seems nice
as a serenade but devdas gets on the nerves
and never outta the rut

in quaint camps in beachy towns,
the potter-turned-sculptor-artist
to be whose muse would be flattering,
he, however, now prefers the marble
because i am not still, can't stop chattering

last in line, the rich daddy's boys
looking for their mummy kinda girls

that's a line difficult to toe
especially since you picked me up
drunk in a club

and you can't scream at me
if you can't understand or reconcile
that it's equally difficult to eat rice with your hands
as it is with a fork and knife

sigh! these hetero people find each other
by what chance or is it sheer numbers?

all i want is to be intimate
with a man i deeply hate
it seems too much to ask
my heterosexual romance

RAQEEB RAZA

Raqeeb is a photographer and research scholar of English literature based out of Delhi. He fanboys over Kamala Das and Sylvia Plath. His works have been published in *Cosmopolitan India*, *The Quint*, *Homegrown*, etc.

What Does It Take to Belong?

Dear brother from Kashmir
You're not the only Pakistani in Hindustan.

My 'Mallu' friend, I've been told,
is now a Pakistani too,
as are all the cow eaters,
or even those, who do not pray
to the 'Gau Mata', they say,
are now Pakistani.

It's an easy qualification nowadays.

And there are others –
Bengalis who do not worship Rama
are from Pakistan
Children of the 'Seven Sisters'

also might as well be,
and students (that damned tribe!)
who protest their own devastation
are Pakistani.

Men who love men
are Pakistani. The untouchables,
refusing to clean themselves, are Pakistani,
and those cursed news channels,
questions still rolling pretentiously in their tickers,
are Pakistani.

It comes down to this:
those not cursing Pakistan
after every Indo–Pak match are Pakistani.
Obviously. No need to retort.

Don't forget
the old word 'dissent'
now carries a Pakistani passport.

HADI HUSSAIN

Hadi Hussain is a social researcher and activist based in Lahore, Pakistan, who is continuously struggling to resist, exist, indigenize and decolonize. His interests include world history, Islamic discourses, intersectional politics, feminism, South Asian LGBT discourse, body politics, cultural anthropology, peace initiatives, decolonization studies and transnational indigenous social movements.

Fat Talk

Once upon a time
there was a man who wrote
long, endless, angry, sweaty, heartwarming poems
all in his head

He wrote on his birthday,
'I wish I could have died
instead of getting older another year.'
Do you know what this means?
Like, what it really means,
when a fat brown gay guy is
continuously at war
with the demons
we call insecurity,

low self-esteem,
body image,
lack of self-love?

He decided to throw that much-cherished-box-of-10-condoms
        which was supposed to be used for fucking
like, for STI-free HIV/AIDS-exempted fucking
        (as if penetration is the only form of sex)
distributed by the NGO which instantly starts shitting
        rainbows, every time there is someone significant
from the western neo-liberal funding machine around,
        shows them through graphs and numbers,
how many condoms and lubes, they have distributed
        among the 'community members' so
                they can fuck safely.

He was one among those proclaimed hundreds of 'members',
who have been reduced to nice
PowerPoint presentations
ensuring white tears of accomplishment,
human rights and
Euros.

Among all the staged activities to woo donors,
        no one there ever talked about –
how to live, and love, how to be desired, to feel
        sexy, how every single body is beautiful,
how every single body must
        be taken care of.

He's the same fat brown gay guy
who is silenced every time he talks
about fat shaming. Or low self-esteem.
Or body image. And of absence of love.

Someone always suggests –
'fit in yaar,
        just lose weight.'

Someone always says how funny it is
        to even talk about such 'issues',
how *he* has a broken sense of humour
        for not laughing at his own fatness. *Laugh Yaar.*
How body image isn't
        a fat-centric issue, and at times
'fatness can be a privilege''not an actual
        struggle' like persons with physical or mental disabilities.
Someone is out there in La-La-Land with a fat fetish
        and he still has a chance to be fucked.

Or how the hell he being an activist,
can feel so low and crappy and shitty and sad and drained
about all this. Other folks look up to him.

As if talking
about a fat brown gay body
which deserves to be loved and desired
is like waging a war against everything
we have been told

The yardstick, to put it mildly, is fucked up –

people fail you
suggest you're useless
in comparison to those
who are also trying

and competing
  and fucking
    and loving
      and living
        and dying
          at the speed of light.

Only if you were to say

You are epiphany
running in my veins.

I realised during the cold nights of *Poh* and *Magh*
with the headstrong incalescence of desires, satiated,
fuming with coals, fragrant
with sandalwood that

only if you were to say,
I'll assemble all the stars
written, painted and sculptured
by every single writer, painter and sculptor,
right to your feet;
illumining all paths
where the dark night of *hijr*
is lamenting,
it will disappear,
I will meet you.

Only if you were to say,
I'll sacrifice my life
caged in this mortal body,
disloyal to me even when
you were around, how it will ever
stay faithful in your absence?
Living has been an extraordinary struggle,
and dying, love stricken.
If you were to say, I'll forbid flowers

to be tender, all drizzle
to be hailstorm.

I'll take on the guise of a prophet,
I'll blow down the Himalayas, the Karakoram, the Hindokush into
      pieces;
set sail to the turbulent waves of the Indus, the Ganges, the Yamuna;
wander around, parched in the Thar, the Thal, the Cholistan
and appear for all the trials and tribulations of
Punnu, Farhad and Majnu,
with results in my favour only.

But only
if you were
to say.

SUDHENDU CHATTOPADHYAYA

Sudhendu is a software engineer by profession and a student of Indian music. He is also an 'emotional writer'. Gender for him is only a label that one has to assume in society but identity is a personal journey for him, the complexities of which he tries to express through his writings.

The Flute

It was 6 a.m. in the morning when the cawing woke me up.

By the time I sat with the tanpura,
the pigeons had already gathered in the balcony.
My voice was croaky as usual;
the audience started their slow brooding.
With a final hauq I managed to croon a clear *Sa*
and received some encouraging flaps.

The teacher's words came back to me.
'You are a bit sharp' was her retort.
She asked the child to sing.
His voice, a soft husky conch,
made me think of a rill breaking quietness somewhere.
I remembered the old family record

that had me chirping like a young nestling.
It had you too…
like thin curls of smoke
burning out of a joss stick.

Once when I had tried to woo a cuckoo,
imitating its plaintive search, you had stopped me,
saying that I was deluding the lovers.
So I had gone back to imitating yours.
The class-teacher had liked it back then.
He let me sing in the choir,
he said it blended well with the girls'.
And just to prove him wrong,
I tried singing louder than all.

When I reached the *Nishad*,
I seemed to miss the pitch yet again.
I looked imploringly into your dove-shaped eyes.
You stood silently holding your flute,
Your eyes cast down.
Even then, you seemed like a memory
of an inanimate past…
Suddenly I heard the cuckoo back in the balcony.

I ran for him
and fluttered into the sky.

ABHYUDAY GUPTA

Abhyuday talks equally feverishly about literature and everything queer and is uncertain about almost everything except his penchant for poetry. He writes about his mental health, queerness, gender and identifies as agender/non-binary. He works as a learning specialist with an interest in behaviour and organizational design. He lives in New Delhi.

Bildungsroman

When I was a child my greatest worry
about growing up was chest hair.

I was scared that they would dance
like unruly monsters
and threaten to out me
as a man.

When I heard about puberty
I did not ask for a deeper voice
or bushy calves but just about anything
else to validate my existence.

In the life before this
I never made it to adulthood.
The story played out till I soaked it in my bones
and told myself I'd make it through this time.

Growing up is like the ache
of the attic floor which squeaks
at the slightest touch
and dissolves into a wallflower to
apologize for its insolence.

Some days I am the attic floor.

On other days
I regret I made it this time.

CHANCHAL KUMAR

Chanchal Kumar is from Jharkhand and currently lives in Delhi. His poems have previously appeared in *The Sunflower Collective, Hamilton Stone Review, Welter Journal* and *Young Poets Network* and forthcoming from *Fulcrum: A Journal of Arts and Aesthetics.*

For Shirin

I try to interpret the messages from when we first met
to predict where it is that we'll find ourselves in at the beginning of
    dawn.
I don't discover many conceits except that maybe
you are the clay bird-bath my old landlord once
placed at the corner of the terrace wall & forgot all about it
(for pigeons to cool themselves and drink from).
I guess someone created you to watch over dilapidated medieval
    architecture –
The queerest patron saint of K-pop and chai-points in the nooks of
    Vijaynagar.
Sometimes we walk till we reach the edge of our worlds
and there's nowhere left to go.
Each person must either be a prison or an island.
Always there exists a *casus belli*

the slightest hint of a century-old rain.
Blue flowers have sprouted quietly from the spots
where our bodies have accidentally touched.
You can't talk about poverty/poetry, you can only live it.
I draw concentric circles to mark my possessions
you point out areas of sleep apnea,
never admitting to being in places other than your home.

ABHISIKTA DASGUPTA

Abhisikta (Obhi), thirty and an aspiring adult. Queer and kinky. Also, a doggie. Lives with her partner in a house that has warm white walls and a room for friends and community to fill in. Loves to cook!

Pleasure JUNKIE

I want to
Obsess
over you

as does

the nine yards of
Blue
around my waist

***

Another pretence
akin to love

I peel off my skin

and like a snake
I rest

***

We drape but
Darkness

with a little make up

and we dance
till our limbs are hairy again

MARY ANNE MOHANRAJ

Mary Anne Mohanraj wrote *Bodies in Motion* (Finalist for the Asian American Book Awards) and fourteen other titles. Mohanraj is a clinical associate professor of fiction and literature at the University of Illinois. She serves as executive director of both *DesiLit* and *The Speculative Literature Foundation*.

After Pulse

His father said: he saw two men kissing
in the street, and it made him angry.

I was eighteen the first time I
spent the night with another girl,
walked back to campus with her
the next morning, wanting to hold
her hand, afraid to.

This is what I was afraid of:
that my parents would somehow hear,
that they would stop speaking to me
would cut me off. That my sisters,

friends, would turn away, repulsed
by thoughts of what two girls might do.

There were incidents on campus.
Gay-bashing, injuries. We wore pink
triangles in solidarity, passed them out
on campus, asked our straight professors –
please. Stand with us. Many did.

Matthew Shepard, a student, was tortured
and murdered a few years later, in 1998.

I didn't think anything would happen
to me. I reached out and took her hand
or maybe she reached out to me. Kissed
her goodbye, knowing already that it
was over, not regretting anything.

Later, my friends and I went to the gay
nightclubs and danced, the straight girls
glad to be able to dance as freely and
sexually as they wanted, without fear
of harassment. I danced on a table, hoping
the gay boys knew, somehow,
that I was one of them.

Twenty years ago; now I'm a wife and mother –
husband, two kids, a dog, and a house

in the suburbs. Still bi, and poly too, but
living as safe a life as one might wish for,
as parents might hope for their children.

The death toll rises, now up to fifty dead,
the worst mass shooting in American history
the worst mass murder of gay people in America
since 1973, Upstairs Lounge, thirty-two burned.

I took her hand, and later, madly in love, I kissed
my girlfriend in the street, knowing always
that it might make someone passing by
angry. In love and defiant, knowing enough to worry.

I didn't know we'd have to worry about this.

Sex After Kids, 2012

a woman asked me yesterday
how is sex after kids?
she had read an essay I wrote
silence and the word
about being a sex writer
about still having trouble
talking in bed.
sometimes the words fail you.
I didn't have a good answer for her
at that moment, but here
is what I would say now.
when I was twenty, I was
a live wire, humming with sex;
almost anyone could have me
if they knew enough to ask;
sex came off me in waves
like heat, like flame.
I was incandescent.
and I won't blame the kids entirely
but for years after them I told people
my sexual orientation was tired.
that live wire was wrapped in layers
of insulation, and buried deep
beneath the surface of diapers
and laundry and dishes;
it's hard to think sexy thoughts
when you're covered in vomit.

now sex is a process of excavation
and it takes a dedicated digger
to peel away the muffling layers
to uncover the naked wire.
but thank god, thank god
when finally laid bare
it still sparks and blazes
incandescent.

CHANDRAMOHAN S.

Chandramohan S. is an Indian English Dalit poet and literary critic based in Trivandrum, Kerala. *Letters to Namdeo Dhasal* is his latest poetry collection.

Love in the Time of CCTV

(i)
'In my rear view mirror is the motherfucking law' – Jay Z

The camera tells us –
keep your hands where I can see them.
Now write your love letter.

(ii)
'Of lovers whose bodies smell of each other' – T.S. Eliot

Queer pride march
with cops escorting us on either side,
like every letter of the poem

being odor-tested
for the scent of the other.

Poet's note: The title owes its origin to a submission call by *Northeast Review* edited by Sumana Roy.

SHIKHAR GOEL

Shikhar Goel is a Hindi poet. His poems have featured in several literary journals and websites. Translations of his poems have also been published in English, Marathi and Kannada. Currently, he works as a researcher at Sarai-CSDS, New Delhi.

Field Report

Professor,
rather than describe
those sad museums,
 those broken terracotta
  sandstone figurines, and
    the Mughal coins,
  would be it okay
 if for our field report
I write about
 those two blue seats
  in the last-but-one row
    of the white bus we took.
  Those slightly longer than usual
fingers, thin, would it be fine
for me to expand on them?
 In that kohl-like night

I had collected
        a windowful of stars.
    Would it be okay
  if I pin them into
this report?

Translated from the Hindi by Akhil Katyal

ANANNYA DASGUPTA

Anannya Dasgupta is from the sea-side. She lives and works in Chennai.

Table for one

'Will someone be joining you?' 'No' said I.
'Table for one.' In the fish pool beside me
a Koi swam up, 'unless you count me in.' I,
a bit wry, 'you need a seat at the table?' 'If
you are able,' said the fish. And so, fin, tail,
scale and all, fish drank; I ate. 'This is new to
me,' I said. 'Me too,' fish nodded its head.
Then it was time to go, 'Cool, if I get back to
the pool?' 'Yes,' I said to the disappearing
fish. What more could I wish? We did sit and
eat; for the rest, fish is fins and I am all feet.

Sari, a Ghazal

I ask in the name of all I have withstood let me go.
For my asking will love's neighborhood let me go?

Your fingers laced in mine, you held tight my hand.
How could I have known that you would let me go?

Give me something of yours to take, you took off
your sari to wrap me in, before you could let me go.

If I have tied you up in knots, if I have strung you
in pins, pierced so, my love, you should let me go.

Un-weave from my sinews, un-mix from my blood.
Un-signed my heart asks, will you for good let me go?

KUSHAGRA ADWAITA

Kushagra Adwaita is twenty-something cis-gendered man residing in Varanasi, pursuing his Bachelors in political science from Banaras Hindu University. Pash, Shiv Kumar Batalvi, Uday Prakash, Neruda, Keats and Frost are his favourite poets. Amicable, witty and humorous; often found ranting about his love for books and shoes; he aspires to be read by millions.

We will be lost

you and I,
one day

just like
I lose all my questions, you
lose all your answers,
like our dreams
are lost as soon as we
count them on our fingers, like
the shooting stars, like
the seven colours
of the rainbow
are lost

like Ma's hands once lost
their vigour, like the old Banyan
was lost, and the well, and
the perch in the mango orchard

like the sky's reflection
is often lost, like laziness
loses its step after sleep, like a people
lose themselves, forgetting
their roots

like many
primitive scripts, languages,
cultures and customs
were lost

like many ships
were lost in the Bermuda Triangle,
like the pencils are lost habitually
from kids' pencil-boxes,
like many of my poems were lost
in moving houses

just like these,
one day, you and I will be lost –
to be lost is written in our stars,
to be lost is our Dhamma.

Translated from the Hindi by Akhil Katyal

R. RAJ RAO

R. Raj Rao, who calls himself queer and not gay, is a well-known writer and professor who started writing poetry and fiction in the 80s and 90s and continues to do so. His most well-known work includes the film *BomGay*, based on his poems, and the novel *The Boyfriend*.

Ass

Like Don Quixote
He rides an ass and thinks he's
On a stallion.

Bombay 2

Fumes shit pav bhaji
Skyscrapers local trains rats
Amitabh Bachchan.

Voice

He calls up to ask:
You, sir, are an activist?
Means you are active?

Old Men

He prefers old men
To Hrithiks and Salman Khans.
Old men have breasts.

ANNIKA

Annika studies English literature by day and writes Hindi poetry by night.

My loneliness and I

often sit and try to guess:
if you were gay, it would've been like that,
if you were gay, it would've been like this:

You would've said you were spending
the night at mine, not just as an excuse:
let my mother lead you
right to my bedroom door.

You would've made a mess
across my mouth with your lip balm:
let me build a bridge
across your shoulders with my hair.

You would've forgotten to shave your legs
but remembered not to care about it:
let me struggle to put into words
just how beautiful they were to me still.

You would've chased all my fears
away with a single finger:
let me get lost for hours
between your thighs.

You would've been embarrassed
to see drops of your blood on my sheets:
let me run and wash them
away in a flood of water.

You would have held my hand
in the morning light and laughed:
let the neighbours call us best friends
as I pressed my lips into your cheek.

My loneliness and I
often ask each other:
If you were gay, what would've been?
If you were gay, what could've been.

Translated from the Hindi by the poet

Poet's note: The poem is a queer reimagining of Javed Akhtar and Shiv-Hari's
'Main Aur Meri Tanhai'

FATEMA BHAIJI

Fatema is a writer who occasionally attempts poetry. They can be found stargazing, waiting for an alien invasion or running their queer lit magazine, *Outcast*. Their work has been published by *Daastan* and Signal 8 Press.

Body/Lost in Translation

Body, I am trying to come home to you
but you are a country my passport does not recognize

Body, all these foreign curves beautiful on other women
is an unfamiliar geometry that does not make sense to me

Speaking of sense, I say 'other women' as if it is a *we*
but the other is so strong I am left cold on the outskirts

Body, you feel like a stranger occupying the same space
because I am too polite to ask you to leave

Body, even when you feel like a suffocating amount of *too much*
I am *too afraid* to mark you wrong for the fear of being lost

SUMITA BEETHI

Sumita Beethi is a queer feminist traveller-writer-activist, a cis-appearing, woman desiring, differently sexual, PAGFB, born with urban, middle-class, Hindu, middle-caste privileges. Sumita writes in Bangla, about queer possibilities, queer liveabilities and about her own traveliving (travel+living) experiences.

Rukmini Banerjee is a translator and lover of languages. She struggles to take time out of her mundane work and read fantastic works of fiction. She loves translating poetry and hopes to continue to do it all her life.

you stretch from east to west

i go north to south
this is also how a plus symbol may appear

Translated from the Bengali by Rukmini Banerjee

NISHANT SINGH THAKUR

Nishant Singh Thakur hails from Damoh, M.P. He strives to explore love, hatred, humanity and every such feeling with the beauty of words, a magnificent source for all his 'content' and sarcastic memes. He lives in Bhopal.

Wandering Even Now

Who just stepped out
   from his home
Who just started
   for his home
Who turned around
   to see it
      one more time
& who turned back
   to find, again,
      the city he left behind.
He who lived far
   from his home till now,
   look at how
      he sees a whole city
   in a home, and

he who left to roam
    like a nomad, who is
        wandering even now,
        look at how he sees
    (is it a joy? is it a pity?)
a home in every city

Translated from the Hindi by Akhil Katyal

MINAHIL ABIDEEN

Minahil Abideen is a Lahori queer trans woman, a student and an activist, who can't cis straight. She loves writing, both as a hobby and a job, and is trying to grow as a writer and as a human. She hopes you all are doing fine.

Love in the Time of Dysphoria

Under the wrinkled tree, our shadows move in and out of each other. She holds my hands, I feel her's, warm and soft, but I am not here. Light years between me and her. Something odd. It's keeping me from her skin. It's something about the shape of her nose, so elegant, so thin, and the curve of her lips, so beautiful. Something about her hair, so long. This something about her – so *feminine*. She wears this word like a shadow, inseparable from her, at one with the tree's. I know she understands exactly what I'm feeling. My desire to look like her. It's a shadow inseparable from me. I think she knows this is a need. It swallows me whole sometimes. That's why she doesn't look shocked when I draw my hand back. The shadow expands. When I shiver looking at her with an unfair jealousy. The shadow mutates. A queer hatred that I wear like an ill-fitting body around my soul. A cry for help. A need to be hugged. It must count as the simplest of needs, to be comforted, and told – and each of us must be told – that everything would be fine. She holds my hand again. This time, I don't retract, I hug her tightly, as if a vacuum is eating the air around us, I whisper into her ear, 'I love you and I'm sorry for being like this,' but she, her face is stern, a line is forming on her forehead, as if telling me I have nothing to apologise for. I feel her lips with the hushed tips of my fingers. So, feminine. I kiss her, cupping her face in my palms. She does the same. With a love so piercing, it's a painkiller. It drowns my dysphoria. It swallows my alienation whole. The shadows overlap quietly.

SULTAN PADAMSEE

Sultan (Bobby) Padamsee was born in 1922 in Bombay. He started writing poetry at a young age and learnt Latin and Greek at a Jesuit institute in Kumaoun Hills, before going to England. The second World War brought him back to India. In the last three-and-a-half years of his life, 'he lived the most intensely creative period possible for an artist'. He ended his life at the age of twenty-three.

O Pomponia Mine!

Shall I knot my tie a little more superbly,
O Pomponia mine?
A little more because we dine at the Astoria
To have bubbles in our wine?

You will wear your black, I think,
The new one, made of Agatha's heirloomed lace,
And add a touch of colour to your face
And leave a little on the glass from which you drink.

We shall play it bravely; only,
Pomponia, alone.
We shall never groan
Even if the rolls are hard,

And the prices on the card
Make us feel a little lonely.

Never mind,
I shall touch my tie,
And lie that we are of a different kind.

You will smile back,
A small cry of laughter in your eyes,
Underneath the hair that loves disguise
You will smile back.

They shall never know,
This is the toxin that adds flavour to our life,
Never know
That you are not my mistress not my wife.

VIJAYARAJAMALLIKA

Vijayarajamallika is an intersex person, she is known as the first transgender poet in Malayalam. Her first collection of Malayalam poetry, *Daivathinte Makal*, is part of the postgraduate syllabus at the University of Madras. Rajamallika's second collection of poems *Aaanadthi—Male River* has contributed ten new words to the Malayalam language. Most recently, she has published her autobiography, *Mallikavasantham*.

Dramaturge and social commentator, N. P. Ashley teaches at St. Stephen's College, Delhi. His areas of interest in research are youth culture, new historicism and performance studies. He is also involved in social work for social empowerment and communal harmony in Kerala.

Posthumous

…kept mumbling:
'I am not a he, but a she,
Can't you see my breast?
Am I not a woman? Am I not?'
Donkeys of the forest try catching up, running,
keeping their volume low while singing
though they could
sing aloud.

In the bus
I insist on that front seat
screaming I am a woman.
The left side mirror collapses,
splinters. The woman, standing
holding a baby in her arms,
is appalled.

The horn-type mustache-walah asks:
'Is that man or woman?'
The one sat next to him, strokes his beard:
'Will know when dead.'

'How?' Foreheads frown in curiosity —
'Isn't bathing the body a must
before placing it
on the pyre?'

Translated from the Malayalam by N.P. Ashley

RAHUL KUMAR RAI

Rahul Kumar Rai was born on 19 July 1986 in a village called Paschimpatti, district Azamgarh (U.P.). Rahul is a poet and playwright. He is a Co-founder of 'T for Theatre' theatre company. He has written plays including *Kaali Ghadi, Shoonya Batta Sannata, Outer Dilli, #Supernova* and *Kebab*. His poetry has been published in online journals such as *Guftugu* and *Indian Writers' Forum*.

The Dark Hour

On our way back from the school
you used to wait for me
under the jujube tree.

Seeing you, glum,
I used to run up the tree straightaway.
You, resting your head on your knuckles,
gazing up, waiting for the jujubes
to fall.

Right then, I shook the branch.
It rained jujubes. Others got to them first
always, your hands got
so few.

Quiet, you returned
to your house, preparing
for a new game,
for hide-and-seek,
for kabaddi –
I was always the parrot
and always, you set off to save me.

Always
you failed.

You were afraid
I'd become someone else's bird.
Wearing your need to win,
you went back home
tried harder.

One day, finally
you were able to free me.

We felt so much pride that day,
both of us.

But should I say something,
that day, right in the middle of the game,
you broke your breath.
No one got to know.

Only I know, and
today – as dusk falls –
I'm letting you know.

Translated from the Hindi by Akhil Katyal

BARNALI RAY SHUKLA

Barnali Ray Shukla is an Indian writer, filmmaker, poet. She has one feature film to her credit as writer-director, two documentaries, two short films, a book of poems, *Apostrophe* (RLFPA 2017). She lives in Bombay with her plants, her books and a husband.

The King Would Send His Men

In another time, in another life,
        they would call those embers, eyes

Eyes that spoke in bold italics
brimming with kohl
kohl that wore silence
bore songs like vapours
of your breath on linings
of silver that held clouds
of doubt in my breast
the king would send his men

Men to tie his queens to a role
between Mondays and Fridays

wet days and dry days
her days and my days

but we were a country
with no borders, molten stories
with no frays
bare in our layers, in our wraps
before the king scored with us
on torn jasmines of our tiara.

His men nailed our sway, in ways
they tore our faith but we flourished
as we wore cyanide inside us, no
we didn't die, we mapped a country.

We belong to each other
in another time, in another life.

IRAVI

Iravi is the nom de plume of a cis woman who loves good crime fiction, lusts after great coffees (and the darker beers), is thrilled by certain poems (and films), and, umm, likes women. She identifies as feminist, Whovian, and Bombaywali.

collateral

in the context of your shifting
agendas
strategic imperatives
theoretical constructs
that outweigh life
unilateral revisions
of needs and decisions
i am that familiar inglorious thing:
afghanistan iraq
a dammed village under water
a marginalised tribe
a bombed school in gaza
a battered wife

yet
nobody can say you lack compassion
your principles are renowned
you are open to dialogue
you are complex and profound

is this how it happens
between women?
casting aside rules and roles
between endearments poetry politics
old songs sung films seen axioms axed
as affirmations abound
in mail chat sms phone fuck sound surround

then at the height then in the midst
your mind begins its track back even as your lips
just leaving mine travel to my ear
and i hear you say
nothing
not sweet not spent not deeper than words
not silence just nothing that feeds on nothing

and tho' sometimes you say you are there
'brightness falls from the air'
like my hair

well
that's how the cookie crumbles
and that's just the way it goes:
the amazon keeps shrinking
and the kosi overflows

as love gets called a cliché
truths segue into lies
mornings turn bleak and chilly
and the elephant dies

Poet's note: The line in quotes is from Thomas Nashe's poem 'A Litany in Time of Plague'.

Not just Strawberries, by the way

It isn't as if strawberries were new to me –
in childhood, we ate quantities
of the small red ones:
fresh strawberry ice-cream by the lake,
strawberries with cream for dinner,
handfuls of strawberries in between.
And if we weren't in Mahabaleshwar
for the summer holidays,
we'd sit, women and children, at the dining table,
sorting firm from pulpy, clean from muddy,
cutting them (after washing!)
in quarters, halves, thirds,
sprinkling powdered sugar on top
and putting them in the fridge
for later.

Then we started getting the bigger ones
so you had only one layer, not two,
but still, out of memory,
we looked beneath the leaves for more –
those leaves never changed, or those boxes.
And we heard about strawberries at Wimbledon
and sang of summer wine
and strawberry fields.

But I'd never had strawberries in chocolate
that my lover and I melted on the gas,
giggling like schoolgirls

in the absence of a double burner, we were
slipshod but effective;
I'd never leaned cosily against my beloved
as she dipped a cool plump strawberry in the still warm
dark enticing mess,
popping it in my mouth for a bite
and then in hers, I'd never followed
such a lead, yet here I was
feeding and being fed
strawberries
between champagne sips and
chocolate kisses.
It's a wonder the chaise wasn't smeared by our fingers,
lips and tongues and faces.
Strawberries can go to your head.

What do I do now with these strawberries
that have come unbidden? I can make
nothing of them at all.

And as for cheese,
we share a long history of growing up
together:
from cheesy bakes of Amul and gorging on Kraft
to cheese snobbery.
Somewhere in between
it became a glamorous substance,
banned
in our vegetarian household
after my grandfather read about rennet,

a calf liver extract, no less, used to curdle milk!
It curdled our stomachs:
we followed his stern correspondence, feeling proud
when the cheese company confessed
they'd been concealing a crucial component
from a country that revered the cow.
But our tastebuds were hooked, we hoarded
cheeses from abroad
in the 'other' fridge, in steel containers at the back
and ate them surreptitiously.

Later, one travelled,
brought back one's own cheeses
and quickly learnt to pair them
with olives, crackers, wine,
and then came those evenings –
so many, when it seemed they'd go on and we'd go on,
so few, really, now that they're gone –
beginning with cheese-n-wine
(tho' we might start at the end
or at any point).

And now I can't say *cheese!* at all.

Wine, did I say? Let's not go there, even,
let's move on, entirely, from food and drink
to talk of teakwood furniture
or certain poems, of films – some not yet seen,
the act of watching imagined as a pact;
let's talk of trips not taken

to certain and uncertain places
with uncertain, probable graces, of our faces
in photographs; let's discuss lengthy cab rides
from town to suburb, tell stories that go with music
from long ago, or listen to what I play now; let's find
what emerges when you centre the mind,
what the cards portend; let's gossip about old lovers
and friends, let's pretend that time's on our side
and love, unlike this evening,
is not about to end. But that was then
and we are other people, you and I.

If we can speak of things not on the list,
we might converse –
or let's not talk at all.

words

we had words,
my love and I and then
when we ran out of known appellations
for each other,
we made up some
and made up some more
and used them all and used them
again, and yet we never exhausted the store

we never tired
we admired our own inventions
our borrowings and declensions
we were always inspired

the words we coined were not
for any ears (or eyes) but
mine, and hers,
but darling baby sweetheart love
seemed also, strangely,
newly minted and never purloined;
honey gleamed in the lamplight in a small bowl
by itself, or accompanied by a bun
or bunch of grapes or laughingly served
by a bunny all bobs ears white behind;
sugar paired off happily with plum;
sweetie came and went
freely,
sometimes bringing a pie – such

a muchness of sweetness was on our lips,
yet we lapped it up, we never said no
because from sweet
excesses we knew that salt would flow;
and when feelings ran
too deep for words, you,
or maybe I,
resorted to a sigh
which only meant
I'm high, when I'm with you my precious
my heart's delight my joy

then the turn of a page
left me wordless
and breathless, I floundered
when I found speech
and found our words
missing

and in their place only a token
remained: your given-by-others-
and-used-by-the-whole-world
actual name

fragrant as flowers,
its syllables pleasing, its utterance
akin to morning prayer,
but had I used it?
I preferred to keep it close, hold it
within, content to let it be

your signifier when I spoke to others,
while my mind was filled
with our secret words,
but to you
I never spoke your name –
on my tongue it was unfamiliar
to both our ears:
short and sad it emerged, sudden
and resigned, how oddly,
how perfectly it became a synonym for 'the end'.

did you have to deprive me of my whole
vocabulary of nouns,
adjectives, names? I have no words left
which I might use to address another
woman,
assuming I wanted
another woman, assuming
another woman
came...

you must be coining new names for
her
that, too, are not for alien ears,
so if I asked you to tell, you would
rightly refuse –
but which of our words do you now re-use
for your newly minted
love?

SHRUTI SAREEN

Born in Varanasi, Shruti Sareen graduated in English from I.P. College, Delhi University. With a keen interest in Indian Poetry in English, she went on to do MPhil and PhD at DU and teaches whenever she has a job. Her poems and short fiction have appeared in South Asian journals. She is currently working on her debut poetry collection.

Baidew

You said I remind you of your sister
when she was very young.

Sometimes I think I could've been
your littlest sister, could've played
with you, read with you,
grown up with you.

Sometimes I think I could have been Axomiya.

I look at your sister – she is like you
but not a mirror image.
Sometimes I think I could be her.
        I could be her sister too.

You, her,
me too.

I could sister-love you, sister-look-up-to-you
and sister-tease you then.

I could've taken that as fundamental fact
before I took on the world.

Sometimes I think I could've
called you
Baidew.

AMMAR HAMMAD KHAN

Ammar Hammad Khan is an Irish-Pakistani student currently resident in the United Kingdom. He has published his own poetry anthology, *Purple Ulcers*, in 2017, and also runs a blog, in order to help current high school students studying literature in English. He is interested in law and literature.

Do You Ever Just?

Do you ever just
pull up a seat in your
rotten four-seater car
and drive to a nowhere
that has nobody
except for a someone:
a pastor, a walking dog, a tired
old mat? Do you ever
just pull up, screeching
the tyres, air conditioner wailing
to wait for a coming? Silently sitting,
drops of sweat drawing you a new face
a plasticky mahogany?
Do you ever just pull out a cigarette
look at yourself in the rear

view mirror, heave in and heave out,
breathe in and breathe out?
Do you ever just watch
your mouth, teeth turning
tainted, a clinical yellow
right in front of your
temporary torn eyes? Wet
as a water jet, yes eyes
breathe in liquid,
my dear. But, when
I think of you, what
I remember is only your
dry breath,
dull horns.
And when you finally decide
to pass through the purgatory
of this moment, does your mouth
not clench at the dried up sweat
that has by now chalked its mark
on you?
Do you, do you ever just...
just think of me?

AGAM BALOONI

Agam grew up in Dehradun, India. 'Meal Planning' is his first published poem.

Meal Planning

I've made rice. Da'ling, come.
Let me order a pair of chopsticks.
No we'll go to Korean *gurocery* store in Delhi
and get us sticky rice to eat it with.
Do buy bedgi mirch tonight for my Thai Curry first
it's got colour but doesn't burn
and you must fry my thighs in batches, please.
The temp'll go down on you fast
and make 'em real moist not crisp.
Ah, in the balls we can put coriander
the parsley was days old, and the curly one's
all sass and no savour
and we could finish our sauce with malai –
it'll be just like cheese.
But first for breakfast we'll do filter kapi yeah?
Thick decoction served with French omelette for Monsieur.

No I shall have mine with a P B J.
Oh I am slobbering now
you've got me all excited.
But wait what're we doing tomorrow for the guests?
Yeah let's do Dominoes and Coke.

I. SAYED

I. Sayed is a queer poet and writer who moves through the Great Lakes, Bengal Delta and the Great Plains.

Only the Wind Can Swing

Only the wind can swing
around buildings in this city,
you cannot sway
your hips down the street or keep
your hair long, you know, *manush ki bolbe,*
meyeder moto lage.
You pull the curtains
until they overlap,
you imagine you're dancing – the mirror shows you're tiptoeing,
afraid the bariwala uncle will hear your bodmashi.
A block away from the mosque, you see two rickshawallahs sleeping –
one's head over the other's chest, bony limbs
entangled like shirtless grasshoppers atop a metal frame.
You skip on your way home but you cannot tell a soul what you saw
and your ribcage gets heavy with untransmitted happiness.
You go to botanical garden, pick and place
flowers in your head and dust them off as soon as they've found
their places.

You take off the silver bangles, and hear
their absent clinking when you lower to tie your shoes.
Around every corner in addas, you hear
that dreadful question: are you married?
You want to talk about water and earth
and about the krishnochura trees that developers uprooted.
But you are, just are, without wanting to be, made to be, a *bangali
mosolman purush*.
You get fed up so you pull out a yellow pad and raise your pen.
You can't decide if you should call the prime minister a goddess
    instead, then
choose to keep it conventionally colonial:
Respected madam,
I implore you to pass a legislation declaring it a criminal offence to
    ask people
about their marital status or marriage prospects except when
relevant interlocutors have established close friendship and can accept
any answer to this question as a valid decision.
I implore you, in addition, to pass an ordinance encouraging
people to inquire about the whereabouts of the
trees and rivers that have gone missing from our cities.
Sincerely yours,
Subject 377
Later you notice an envelope under your door.
Inside – a blank page.
Could they not read your letter?
You try heating the paper over a flame – no, nothing.
You hold in front of your face the paper's indifference to your
    difference.
You put the paper under your pillow,

place it on the desk,
fold it and keep it in the drawer.
You hover through alleyways and bedrooms
with the letter in your pocket.
You trick yourself into feeling acknowledged in the letter's illegible
    presence,
and get used to living in the space between desires and dictatorship.
You talk about yourself in the second person because
you've learned to see yourself as an/other.
Today, today though, you claim yourself.
Yes, you say I, and I declare I read this poem to you as I myself
from the blank page in my pocket.

AMAL RANA

Amal Rana is a queer Pakistani Muslim poet and arts educator based out of unceded Musqueam territories in Vancouver, Canada. Her poetry has been nominated for a Pushcart Prize and appears in numerous journals and anthologies. Amal collaborates with multiple communities to vision decolonial futures through the arts.

Janazah for Pulse

> *'Gazing at so many billions of brilliant stars, it's hard*
> *to know which formed at the beginning of time,*
> *and which burst into existence last week.'*
> Ross Anderson, *The Atlantic*, 16 November 2015

On Laylatul Qadr
the night during Ramadan when Allah is closest
and the angels are said to walk amongst us
I pray for you

Inna lillah wa inna ilaihi raji'un

I look up duas and surahs not uttered in years
knowing tonight they will be multiplied into thousands

Future ancestors taken too soon
you are not a requiem
you are stars
in existence before the beginning of time

Stepping out under crescent skies
dusk finally agreeing to break my fast
I look up first for your radiance dancing across the galaxies

In scientific terms when celestial bodies make noise
they call it 'stellar music'
I swear I hear the strains of reggaeton
my hips swivel into the different rhythms of all our ancestors
whispering
'our stars in heaven hallowed be your names'

POOJA AND TEENASAI

Pooja (Jo) and Teenasai are a non-binary gay couple from south India. While Jo is a social researcher who is on their way to a PhD, Teenasai is an indie musician and goes by the monicker GrapeGuitarBox. They both find comfort and strength in activism, and fighting alongside each other.

Games

April:
Don't make me think about the time
you linger right above my panties
your nose against the cotton
breathing in my entire being
before shifting it aside,
your index finger running up and down
feeling the wetness, next to your thumb
over my clit, softly then firmly
I whimper in your ears
tell you to please, please, please
I beg you to take me
and with one stroke, you enter me,
I arch my back for you

you put me in your lap
like something to feast on
and savour me
you look at me like I own the world
and you are touching it inside me.

May:
Oh, the games we play
we play them in places
no one can see us.
We play to a scoreboard
that turns our hearts into dust.
We wrestle gently
laughing and rolling
our bodies pressed together
whispering a sweet sound,
my fingers trace your back
my tongue finds its way
you dig your nails into my skin
all that matters is now & today,
I reach where I have to
where the light beckons me,
your whispers turn into moans
that follow my rhythm slowly.
Nothing else matters when it feels
like our souls are exploding within.
Oh, the games we play,
we both always win.

WARM ME

Warm Me is a person who sometimes wants to be AI who sometimes wants to be a person. They are interested in landscapes, cityscapes and body-scapes. They do not wish to be identified, they do not wish to be remembered, they do wish for eternal summer.

Love Notes for Druids

It began with:
    a house is not a space
it is a series.

Sometimes, in search of you
    I enter an image
it has a flat coir mattress
    a glimpse of a secluded corner
and many other dimensions
    only known to the two of us.

In that series
    I'm the only one who can see
listen to ambient sounds
    feel a faraway pull of distress
an eclipse controlling
    all the fluids in me.

I am dreaming of you
    but we were not perfect
almost never a calling
    just an enchantment
like a leaf is to a tree
    wearing warning signs
of an upcoming storm.

I am yet to enter another series
    another 'home' I have yearned for
surrounded by dry-wood
    encased in tar
this image forms endlessly
    and begs you to enter it with me.

When I re-tell this story once again
    describe this image
you can defend its magnificence
    there sure will be shit-talk
a dampness drawing closer
    to this victorious body I've created
for the meek, the unwanted, the sullen.

This image is composite
    made of compounds
known neither to you nor me
    as this data drips into my pores
and coagulates, I can see us get high.
    I accept that like every other you
too will not return to that house.

SAM(IRA) OBEID

Poet. Indian. Activist. Lesbian. Scholar. Warrior. Sam(ira) Obeid was born and raised in Chennai, India. She moved to the U.S. when she was twenty-three becoming an intersectional resistance activist/poet who speaks to the tensions of immigration, gender and sexuality. She loves fashion, martial arts, the outdoors and her pitbull, Sherlock.

Genderfuck(ed)

There is nothing here
There is nothing here but a blank slate
There is nothing here but flesh and blood and skin and bones
And then
      she appears

She stands here naked for the first time
Body scarred with violence she has not yet feared
Face lined with stories she has not yet told
She stands here naked, for the first time too long
Crouched, cringing, waiting for cover
Her Muslim heritage has taught her well
That this body is no ground for pride
And then
      he appears

He stands here naked, for the first time
Clenched fists covering her breasts
Spine erect, butch present

He stands here naked for the first time too long
He is nothing without the absence of her
She is no one without the fallacy of him
Together
        they become

The thing about identity is we're always ready
To check each other into boxes
Even when there's no paperwork to be done

I am an independent woman
But one of my closest friends sees it fit to call me sexist
When I say I am uncomfortable
Being financially supported by a significant other
Even though I have no problem
If she decides she doesn't want to work a day in her life

I ask her to think about what she's just said
If maybe I looked more feminine
She may have had a different opinion or
If maybe she would've respected the independence
I learned at a young age
I must never give up
By consequence of being a woman

We are both women
I just wear mine differently than
      you yours

There's a compulsory misogyny that comes with this identity
That can be so blinding you completely miss the point
So quick to label me in your own image
All of a sudden I am not woman enough to understand
All of a sudden I am not my mother's daughter
But my
      father's son

The thing about identity is we are always ready
To tell someone who they are
So we can see ourselves in them
Universe forbid we should ever say – 'I don't understand
Tell me more,' so when I do
It appears I impose my identity upon you

Please know I am not honored by the look of surprise on your face
When I tell you my pronouns are female
Please know
I am not honored
by the look of surprise on your face
When I tell you consent applies to me too

Human nature requires that we destroy that
Which we do not understand

So we take difference and fix it into a box
One size fits too small – we peel back its skin
and rip through its flesh, until we break
its every bone and bleed it soaking wet

Until there is nothing here
There is nothing here but a blank slate
There is nothing here but flesh and blood and skin and bones
Until
      we disappear

DIBYAJYOTI SARMA

Dibyajyoti Sarma has co-edited the queer anthology, *Whistling in the Dark* (2009) with R. Raj Rao, and has published three volumes of poetry and a work of translations, besides writings in edited volumes and journals, including *Out!* (2012). He was born in Assam and now lives in Delhi, where he runs the independent publishing venture Red River.

There was nothing common between us

I was young, he old
I was rustic, he sophisticated; I poor, he rich
I restless, he rooted.

We spoke different languages.

The only thing that worked was mysterious, was absurd. Sometimes we called it 'love'.

I was happiest in his company –
when his old fingers caressed my restless hands

when my thumb recognised his hungry lips when we got drunk and
ambled on the empty streets at midnight
with my arm around his shoulder

when he drove and I craned my head to his bosom
when he said 'I love you' to me in Tamil
when I fell asleep to his heartbeat.

Fifteen years later, I still miss the heartbeat.
I close my eyes and I can hear it.
I cannot endure.

There was nothing common between us.

We knew the night will end soon.

So I started collecting memorabilia – a photograph of us, his visiting
card, the number of his car on a piece of paper safely tucked in my
purse, a packet of half-smoked Marlboro, the audio cassette of Iruvar
because it was his favourite, an ushanka he got me from Russia, an
empty bottle of Royal Challenge, a box of dark chocolate in the shape
of the Singapore Lion. I started memorizing the details of his life, his
phone number, the name of his father, and the name of his first lover,
the neighbourhood in Chennai where he grew up, all the places he
had travelled to, his mother's death anniversary and the name of her
household god.

It was inevitable –

one day I will flee this alien City of the Blessed
one day his heart will explode a thousand tiny pieces in a sky-blue
hospital room.

So we built a relationship on the road, between a restaurant and a
hostel, in a car.
At midnight.

*

He loved me too much to let me see him wither away.
I wasn't allowed the hospital visits.
All I could do was to make a call at 11 a.m.

That month, all my days were 11 a.m.

Then the calls stopped.
I was promised I will receive a call once he was out of the hospital.

Three months later, I got the news.

SEHRISH RASHID

Sehrish Rashid is a bisexual woman from Pakistan, who now lives in the USA. A single mother, constantly exploring her identity and relationships as a brown, queer, Muslim woman in a heteronormative world. Takes pride in Urdu, and is trying to contribute to this world through her words and actions.

Maaz Bin Bilal is the author of *Ghazalnama: Poems from Delhi, Belfast, and Urdu* (2019), and the translator of Fikr's Taunsvi's *Chhata Darya* from Urdu into English as *The Sixth River: A Journal from the Partition of India* (2019). He is Associate Professor of literary studies at the liberal arts school of Jindal Global University.

Shame

Do I keep your shame?
Do I uphold your name?
Why don't I taste the flame
of the desires kept locked up for an age?

They say it's a tale from yesterday,
but I swear on my loneliness,
this story is very old,
that had to be hidden
suppress with many stratagems,
would not be told,
then why today, again,

should I let the fragrance
of this hereditary secret
be covered by the blanket
of your rotten soul?
Do I keep up the show?

If those shame and honour,
piety and sin, of yours,
are hidden in my
preference, my sex,
then these are kinks of
your brain,
don't make them a collar
for my neck,

In this white versus black war
of yours,
In these right and wrong colours
of yours,
why should I tire
with you?

This is the fight of your prison
Don't make this a thing about my soul.

What for you is a thing of shame,
only spells my truth, my name,

Why should I rethink it for you?

This is my time to fly,
Then why should I stay with you?
Why should I keep
your shame for you?
Why should I uphold
your name for you?

Translated from the Urdu by Maaz Bin Bilal

SANTA KHURAI

Santa Khurai, a nupi maanbi from Manipur, a south-eastern Himalayan state in the Indo–Myanmar border. Nupi maanbi can be translated as indigenous Meetei transwoman. An artist and activist, Santa works with All Manipur Nupi Maanbi Association (AMANA).

The Second Women Or The Nupi Maanbi's Thabal

Breasts fitted
Some with soft sponge, some with water-filled condoms
Arched eyebrows akin to that of a bow
Fine shaped lips, murky eyelids, cheeks pink with rouge,
Thick false eyelashes, which when closed, seemed
Like black bees seated on budding lotuses,
As in our words, *'Apomba thambalda aamuba khoimuna tongba'*
Forming hordes, they plunged into the battle
'The Second Women.'
In their minds, each thought,
I am the most beautiful of the lot –
Gorgeous. Striking. Invincible. Idolized by all.
In every corner of the battlefield
They downed the spirit of courage
The stench of the fluid mingling with the red colour of their lipsticks

An amorous odour coursing through their veins
of envy, of longing, of passion.

Music –
Drums. Saxophones. Lights.
Greeting their arrival
Spectators throng at the battlefield
Enjoyed, applauded and judged the warriors
How fortunate the second women?
So many spectators did not gather in the battle of the sexes in
    your world
With each drumbeat, a peg of the armour fluid
In a moment
The fluid flooded through the sensitive nerves
Pursuing them to the conviction of present
No history, no dreams but only the 'Now'
Life began at evening and end in dawn
Music began and commenced the scuffle
Every troop one warrior and four to five foes
Music stopped within the limited time
But the wrestling carried on till the dawn
Somewhere in the corners.
The war over, homewards bound then
'The Second Women.'
On the way back to their homestead
In the silence of the night
Laughing with ecstasy
These Goddesses of the Dark
One to another retold the story of the battle
Women with worn out lips, the red colours smeared

One with the lashes missing on an eye
Another one with her shapeless breast
Yet in silence were the defeated in that battle
The second women discerned it
The eastern horizon about to light up
The exhausted bodies embraced rest
The moment they closed their eyes
The questions rang constantly in their mind –
Who are we?
What is the purpose of our lives?
Are we in the real world?
Atrocious questions trapping them in their bloodcurdling lives
Tears fell down silently in agony
Each women's eyes brimmed over
Yet none told the other
The tears flushed away the stories of that battle
Snoring and dozing they fell asleep
Waiting for the next battle...

My Father

My hand wrapped around his finger, he taught me to walk
With pride, flaunted me to the world
Shared his future with me
With the dream, I'd reinstate his position
I as a 'FATHER' and he as a 'GRAND FATHER'
The wind of changes visited
And disturbed the hopes, dreams and beliefs
My dolls provoking him
The female vocal code insulted the innocent fatherhood
My teacher who taught me the ways of the world
Abandoned me without sympathy
My temperament transformed him into a demon
But I ... I was neither a traitor nor a liar
The more the truth provoked him, the more he strove to impose
The farthest belief which my tender mind could ever reach
My heart throbbed at the scenes –
The torn dolls, the broken casket, the harsh warning voice
Demarcation of man and woman
Forced the effeminate to shoulder 'manly' responsibilities –
Dig, cultivate, harvest and mend fences.
Croakily my father roared out his wishes
Bamboo baton and the hard palm welcoming me
My lamentations and wails went unheard
All and sundry commented dreadfully
'ABNORMAL, HOMO, BLACK SHEEP and BAD OMEN'
These memories of my childhood created the demon in me –
Mind filled with hatred, disgust and revenge
Even as I found irresistible those of my same kind.

Time then took him away from my life
The grey hair, missing tooth and weakened body
He lay now on a white loin cloth that matched his height
Nose fitted with two small cotton balls
Breathless, lifeless, he lay in the middle of the courtyard
Kids and kin forlornly mourned for the dead
In the midst, these kind-hearted human kind
Counselled me to wear 'PHEIJOM'
Hearing it I felt
As if I was bathing in a pond filled to the brim with the *tillaikhombi*.
The slim bond of love for my father, the pangs of losing him,
Everything vanished in a moment.
Started looking for exit, the kind humans compelled me to refrain
   from the angst
Fresh wall was built between the dead and my gender.
He was burned at the crematorium
The place where many women too were consigned to fire after they
   died
There he went thus, leaving no legacy of his own gender
Without leaving behind a separate cremation ground for men.

ASH SAL

Ash Sal is a part-time wallflower and full-time feminist.

Against Biology

The pocket is an element I often find myself reaching for out of instinct; always I find that the structure of my kameez does not carry anything other than my body. The history of pockets, after all, is the history of potentiality, the possibility of need, being, in a place other than home; the history of pockets, after all, is the history of movement across space.

A woman's lap in Urdu is named *goud*, which, now transliterated, sounds oddly divine. God, goud, women: the family of cradle, where things born are kept and grown.

May pockets sprout on laps! – is my prayer following the memory of two women slouching on chairs facing each other. Their legs lounge in birthlessness. I hear their howl, the ungraceful scrape of sneakers against the ground as their bodies shift to rhythms of conversation. My memory of not being able to name them in the language of family; I think they have pockets on their shirts.

Or at the very least, I imagine one of them wearing a *patiala*; the history of *patiala* is the history of a royal dress becoming feminine over time. A rallying cry for the appropriation of the royal dress code! – is my thought following the memory of a woman who demanded life, stole it, with stealth, in danger, from the hands of men.

Cradles that nurture the filth of life, trinkets, messy, unvirtuous, but useful: I hear them, I remember.

The trees of lineage have heavy branches; blood is thick. For instance, my eyes, and face, and mouth will all be a Striking Resemblance.

I would like to, however, plant an additional fruit (even if it hangs rather precariously), which is, I am told, a poem against biology: Women who have birthed my language and laughter. Our lineage will be friends and lovers, who saw our wombs and said, may you be of yourself.

ARINA ALAM

Arina, twenty-six, lives in Coochbehar. She identifies as a woman, is a blogger and a depressed soul in a lunatic mind.

I Know

I know

    in which street I will meet my bullies
    where I will face ridicule
    when unwanted eyes will rip off my clothes, expose my genitalia
    when I will be the victim of a fun-less crowd

I know

    on which corner I will hear whispered speculations
    about my gender

But I don't know

    when I'll be smacked because my androgynous face disturbs
    haters
    when petrol will be poured and lit because my rapist thinks
    raping a eunuch   body is disgusting

I know

    which hands will beat me in a crowded train

which hand will try to touch my breasts in a dark corner
which smile will trivialise me, deny my gender
which smile is asking for sexual favours

But I don't know
when I'll lose my mind because of the bullies
when I will take the blade to draw lines on my wrist
when Folidol will seem my only option

I know
when my dysphoria gets worked up
when I dream of fitting my body in my gender like a Rubik's cube
when I escape into my room to avoid the scornful crowd

When I revolt against this construction of gender
I will keep my head held high

I will fly

RUHAIL ANDRABI

Ruhail Andrabi is currently a doctorate student in JMI. He writes for *Creativity and Learning*, *Café Dissensus*, and *Dotism* journal, a blog based in Sydney, Australia. His poetry travels across the cities of existentialism, resistance and gender. He explores metaphysical questions of life through metaphors as they interact with matter and space.

I'm now a butterfly

of poems.

Carrying the dead
      metaphors on my wings,
      broken.

My proboscis will refill it
      as love is emptied
      from the sky.

When autumn falls
      I will bleed an ocean.

This journey has a name:
      solitude.

I have a thousand desires:

to be dust
on the barren south pole
        of the moon

a wanderer who has chanced upon
        the turnpike of your beauty

a grave digger
who for decades
is burying hearts.

I worship the madness
        in your beauty.

Some call it disaster.

Some call it
ecstasy.

PHURBU TASHI

Phurbu Tashi is based in Nepal. He is in his mid-thirties and wishes that queer lives in Nepal, though beautiful, be surrounded by people who are more considerate and accepting.

Rohan Chhetri's first book *Slow Startle* was the winner of the The (Great) Indian Poetry Collective's Emerging Poets Prize 2015. His second collection of poetry won the Kundiman Poetry Prize and is forthcoming in 2021.

This World Isn't for You

They say *This world isn't for you*
Why then was I born into it, if it wasn't for me

You are different, your manners are different too
Where should I go, there isn't a different world for me

This isn't nature's fault, these are your own desires
Why would I embrace desires that make life harder for me

You should be hacked to death and thrown away
Dear lord, by being who I am, what is the worst that I've done

Perhaps this is an age of darkness, that is why the world is so
If 'you' are the house of virtue and innocence
I might as well take all the blame

Don't say this universe is only yours, dear all
Let us not discriminate, but laugh and share joy

This is what I pleaded with all of them!

Translated from the Nepali by Rohan Chhetri

AKHIL KATYAL

Akhil Katyal is a poet, translator and teacher based in Delhi. His third book of poems *Like Blood on the Bitten Tongue: Delhi Poems* came out in 2020.

When Farida Khanum

sings now

she does not hide
the age in her voice

she wraps it in paisleys
instead

and for a moment
holds it in both of her hands

before
drowning it in our sky.

When she sings now
she knows

at the end of that note
when her voice breaks
like a wishbone

he will stay.

SAHAR RIAZ

Sahar, in her own words, 'is a psychiatrist from Pakistan, currently living in Dublin. On my journey to self discovery, I have leaned on poetry, art, philosophy, psychology and literature. I believe that any form of self-expression should be an integral part of everyone's life.'

Do you want to get to know me

or the person whose body I wear?
Smiling like everyone else,
holding inside the charcoal
of sorrow

All day I wait to come home
hang those curves in a hanger
change into my pants and t-shirt
tie my hair up in a bun,
smoke a joint

All day I wait for the night to come
so I can wipe off this mask,
reveal something real,
if only to myself

I know 3 a.m. like the back of my hand

As the hours go by I wonder why
this hurts the most – in a world
where you're shunned for being too fat
too smart, where you're gunned for
a skin too dark or showing who you are
where your wings are set on fire
for flying too close to the sun

How do I survive
this scorching heat? The word 'normal'
is diamond-hard in the palm of my hand.

Maybe we were never meant to live *normally*.
Maybe that word will one day
set fire to itself. Maybe one day,
we will shine like the millions of stars
against a charcoal sky.

PRIYADARSHINI OHOL

Priyadarshini Ohol is a cross-disciplinary, questioning artist. Her practice is rooted in transformation, activism, freedom and play.

Rubbish

Letters, declarations of love, marriage, promises, mementos, gifts, coat-hangers, cards, books, pictures, sweaters, purses, hats, clothes

of a life shared.

I took down paintings, drawings, slogans and posters.

Only their stickies jut out from my bare walls.
Even socks, and a jacket that kept me warm,
a jewellery box and the red camera.
All that I could, I gave back.

The rest was reluctantly given away.

A blanket, remaining clothes,
the pretty yellow summer dress we bought & I gaily wore,
thrown away, dust-binned, left somewhere behind.

Somethings I tore and cried.

I'm moving on.

Met some old friends,
even went on a date.

You would think, everything's been purged
but no. I found your perfume, our forks,
and more of your clothes.

I did the laundry that day.
The black tee with a skull
fluttered in the wind by my window
I smelled it for your scent
and lay in bed, for two days.

When I got on my feet,
I soaked it
in nail-polish remover,
cleaned my nails,
redid them,
then used it to dust my desk.

It's in the bin now
right where it belongs

SHRUTI SONAL

Shruti Sonal is a poet based in Delhi, who loves getting pixie cuts just to annoy her neighbourhood aunties.

The Pixie Cut

The first time I chopped off my hair

the questions came
loud and quick
like bullets
in the air
like I'm a soldier
caught in the cross fire,
with a pair of scissors

Hayye rabba!
Tujhe depression ho gaya hai kya?
said the neighbourhood aunty
at the neighbourhood shop
I laughed and replied
Nahi aunty, meri girlfriend ko pasand hai!

Aunty had an earthquake.

She whispered
names of a thousand gods
under her breath, walked away

I went home, told my mother
We both laughed
She laughed some more
Meri beti lesbian
thodi ho sakti hai

The earthquake, again,
different this time
her words
  the ground
    splitting open
        trembling, not thinking

the boy
I kissed in high school
  the girl
    I'd named stars after
        in return of a kiss

trembling
not asking
but what if she is?

would you then whisper
    names of a thousand gods
        under your breath?

SHAAN MUKHERJEE GHOSH

Shaan Mukherjee Ghosh moved to India from England as a teenager in 2013. Currently, he is an undergraduate student at Lewis & Clark College. He is non-binary and bisexual.

Pantomimesis

There are things you cannot fathom.
This is not about being doped up watching time expand.
Nobody can really fathom the universe expanding, but you can
    imagine.

I tried to imagine my negligence in the universe,
not able to put my finger on how I had this body,
this name, this consciousness and not another's. Not my thoughts,
but my mind itself behaves like a child, uncertain of when to use past
    tense.

How can someone be too young when every moment is their oldest?
I wasn't too young when lying awake at night,
Claudius dripped family secrets into my ear. Later I'd find my blood
    curdled.

You train your voice

like anything else, with punishment and reward.
Wind me up and make me sing until I'm sure I've learned to ignore
    stage fright.

I am gifted and talented. Nobody will call me stupid or lazy.
I would never drink or smoke or have sex before, I'm too young.
Thank god I believe in god and she knows the path that's best for me.
But it can't involve moving to India. I am not like my cousins.

I can't be gay or trans or depressed.
I won't hurt my body even when it hurts me.
I will not abuse others as I have been abused.
Everything I thought was wrong. I suppose I was too young to know.

Only after I knew, these things were always true.
I don't believe in linear explanations of cause and effect any more.
I don't know which is more inevitable:
words sealing my fate or sealing up tape over moving boxes,
Cardboard time capsules with no date set to open them.

The show must go on, although I don't remember learning any of the
    songs.
People tell me I sing well. I don't remember the colour of their eyes.
I am distracted by all the chests buried in my garden.
I treat every tree like the first and last one that has ever grown.
When the fruit shrivels up before it has a chance to ripen
Then I realize that coffins fall apart
and what grows in that ground is contaminated.

Time has built a treehouse out of bricks of my past.

I am surrounded. The branches have been ripped out of context,
but they are more structured in death than they ever were in life.
I almost believe I will never be old enough,
Brave enough, to dig up the lead-lined boxes that nearly killed this
   tree.

My first real monsoon washes away the earth. They sit in the open.
The ground is littered with dead stalks and thorns.
I sleepwalk and for months, my legs are covered in cuts from blades
   of grass.

I still don't know what I am doing when I stand up,
blood drying on my legs like the first time I grasped that this was my
   childhood.
Something pushes me to push the boxes to the side, into the shade.
Somewhere, I register they are far bigger than I recalled.

I knew the seasons had changed when a northern wind started
   blowing.
Sometimes I imagine the boxes are really crates full of fruit from my
   orchard.

But for now they are furniture,
I lean against them to smoke,
knowing that whatever is in them is behind me.

MOKSH

Moksh is a gay man who lives in Mumbai. He is a trainer by profession. His writing started out of the blue one day. He loves travelling, reading, photography and swimming.

That one crime

I'm guilty of a crime
no matter what I do
when I try to forget
I remember you

Translated from the Hindi by Aditi Angiras and Akhil Katyal

ADITI ANGIRAS

Aditi Angiras is a poet, writer and artist based in New Delhi. She is the founder of *Bring Back The Poets*, a queer collective of South Asian poets.

My Mad Girl's Love Song

There are days when I really miss you, Sylvia.
Nights like these I wonder, what if
things were different that one night
and you had met me
at that party. 1956, February 25.
Between the jazz and the poems,
drinking whiskey and ginger wine,
walking on air, like a holy high
you'd stumble and step on my toes
so we'd end up dancing all night.
You'd quote me, my poems
and I'd court you, more poems.
Where you'd not need to be you
confused, inebriated
and I'd not need to be Hughes,
to be huge with the ladies.
I dreamed that you bewitched

me into bed (Oh Sylvia!)
And sung me moon-struck,
kissed me quite insane.
Head in the clouds, you'd got me
singing 'Oh na-na, what's my name?'
Now that we're sober, tell me
Dear Sylvia? Would you still die
with your head in the oven
or, stay, six years later to
hold my hand at the stonewall riots?
Say, won't you write me a poem
to tell me we're real, alive not dead
loving like fuckers, fucking like lovers
so I'd stop feeling that. . .
(I think I made you up inside my head. . .)

CHAND

Chand is a Queer, agender trans research scholar, with a special interest in the intersection of Queer theory and development discourse. They love writing, banoffee pie, their adorable yet mercurial dog Neo, and constantly daydream of a world without gender.

What is Queer?

Sit down, Amma
I have to tell you something.
She looked at me and said
What is it?
I took a deep breath and blurted
Amma, I am queer.
A puzzled Amma asked
What is Queer?
Amma, how do you want me to answer
such a loaded question?
Queer is that momentary hesitation I had
when I was asked if I was even a man
Queer is me averting my gaze when
you talk about my marriage
Queer is me telling you that
marriage is a cisgender-heteronormative institution

Queer is the Tedagadu
the strange gender/sexual variant
who brings destruction to the family
who every Telugu parent warns their child not to be
Queer is the resistance that blocks out
their warnings that will bring
destruction to the family
Queer is the adrenaline rush I felt
when our eyes first met and his lips
were on mine, with every inch of my body set afire
Queer is Nanamma recounting the blood and sweat
shed by our lower-caste weaver ancestors
the sound of their handlooms punctuated
with tears of helplessness
Queer is the magic of the term Bahujan
I have embraced with every fibre of my being
Queer is when I read *Annihilation of Caste*
and marvelled at the sheer force of Babasaheb's arguments
Queer is the moment I realised he left a momentous legacy
a path of salvation, offering hope in this darkness
Queer is the Kajal and bindi that I don
to challenge the binaries of gender and gender itself
Queer is the end of structure
and the resistance to the epistemological violence
Queer is being the lowest of the low
the absolute scum of the earth
the bottom of the sexual pyramid
and somehow still taking pride in it
Queer is the galaxy of endless possibilities
situated just behind those prisons of the binaries

Queer is me realizing I can be everything and nothing
that I don't have to choose
Queer is the driving force that makes me
want to break the fetters I am bound in
Amma, Queer is me
I am Queer, Amma.

GOWTHAMAN RANGANATHAN

Gowthaman Saroja Ranganathan speaks Tamil and Gibberish to cats and dogs. He loves cycling and likes to be in a classroom as a facilitator or as a student. He is pursuing an LLM in Human Rights and Comparative Constitutional Law at the University of Texas at Austin as a Fulbright Nehru Master's Fellow.

As he cleared his desktop

there were snippets of this   and   that.
A lost inspiration, a stunted story, a sketchy vision.
Momentary but momentous.
He wished to tie them up, complete it all.
Instead, he took a deep breath
        deleted it all.

*

On an impulse, they decided
        to romance the city bus that evening.
Standing next to each other,
        placing the bags at their feet,
        they held on to the bars to avoid the inertia

the toppling off.
Stand sideways, not facing the bus,
that way you would cheat inertia.
As the bus jerked, his nose
      buried in his hair, he was comforted
      by the mild shikakai.
They teased and played
      in the midst of a hundred tired bodies.
And somewhere, he let go of the inertia
      to not believe.

*

The tropical wet night
      was conducive for the mosquitoes to buzz.
He struggled to shoo away the ones on his feet
      but not before they left a sting
      and he was left scratching
      one foot to another.
All this in a state of semi-awaked-ness,
      too tired to rise. Then he felt it.
The soothing citronella repellant
      cool and fragrant spread by balm
      tender hands on his feet.
Like a lullaby, soothed,
      he slept.

*

He hadn't felt aroused

or any desire in days.
The viral attack shook his body
made him know
         his fragility.
All he felt was the hand that touched
his forehead every now and then.
A hand that gently pressed the cold compress.
         He saw him in his favourite boxers of theirs,
that moment, the viruses knew they were doomed.

*

He waited for the weather to be pleasant
so that they could cuddle again.
The whole of last month their bodies lay away
like magnets that don't get along.
As the showers cooled down the city,
he realized – the summer could not be blamed.
*

He ran past the aged rain trees
and the wrinkled silk cotton tree.
Darting through Cubbon's deserted paths
         he was determined to outrun fear.
The gentle Bangalore drizzle patted him.
As he ran, he had company –
a mangled mongrel kept pace
         seeking shelter by his side.
The canine feared his fellows
         felt assured in the presence of a human.
Each silently acknowledged the other's fear.

As they emerged, with the first sight of traffic,
       the dog rushed away to safety, letting go
of his fear. He continued the pace breathing out
his fear amidst the silver oak.

*

The chipped red and green walls
stood stripped of the images that once adorned them.
As they patiently peeled off the remnants of the images,
the scarred wall in the barren apartment
stood testimony to their two years.

*

The last two times, he left the city after a break up –
unable to bear the memories stitched to each street.
This time, he stayed. Realizing the city's the one
       he's romancing.
Everything else
was just a ploy.

*

What he wished for the most was a picture of himself
       with his loved one inside one of those cabins
that pull out sketchy images of happy faces;
       the red box in the corner of the mall.
That would be his ritual, a framed photo

with his significant other.
That would complete him, he thought.
But when he realized that 'completion lies within'
he got a sketchy image of his toothy grin,
 put it on his work desk.

*

Over a month passed. No calls
made or received. His phone pulled down
the number from speed dial.
After a brief call today, it bumped the number back
to the top. The phone glared
        with hope.

*

Don't. Told you not to put the phone in your shirt pocket.
        It is harmful for the heart.
Few months after him, he caught himself
putting the phone in the shirt pocket.
The familiar reprimand was nowhere close.
Out of spite, he let the phone be.
        The heart was anyway b r o k e n.

*

The Evocative Song and the Kaleidoscope
spoke to each other after a long time.

When they last spoke, the Kaleidoscope
        was pretty, shiny bangles.
It broke into a hundred pieces hearing the Song.
Now. Years later it has gathered itself into a Kaleidoscope,
flirted with the song yet again.

*

Secrets. The after taste of coffee. Colour. Purple? Weather? Drizzles.
Comforted.   They parted.

RUMI HARISH

Rumi Harish is a transman who has been working on the issues of sexuality and gender rights for the past nineteen years. He is a student of Hindustani classical music, learning under different gurus for the past thirty years. He has also written plays and articles on sexuality and gender issues.

Mamta Sagar is a poet, playwright and translator from Bengaluru. She is conferred with Bhashabharathi Translation Award (2019). *Hide and Seek*, her bilingual poetry collection in English comes with source text in Kannada (2014). Mamta is actively involved with international poetry translation projects. She is associated with the Creative Writing Programme at Srishti Institute of Art, Design and Technology.

the girl-girl affair

yesterday night she returned to the sky
her earrings jingling an invite to my anklets
toward the terrace I followed
standing over the parapet wall, stretching my hands I asked
'what should we call the love we share?'
She stretched her hands and said, 'yes,
let's call our love kanagale the flower'.

little by little I started melting in her embrace
next morning people swarmed in front of the house
'that foolish girl jumped down the terrace and committed suicide
girl-girl affair it seems'

Translated from the Kannada by Mamta Sagar

Translator's note: Rumi Harish traversed his journey as an active feminist singer who walked through lesbian activism and is now a transgender activist engaged with voicing rights for the community. This poem is from his lesbian phase.

RAJORSHI DAS

Rajorshi Das is a queer non-binary poet and researcher. Born and brought up in Kolkata, his poems dwell on the unstable categories of home, desire and friendship. When not writing, you can find him in classrooms, exploring the possibilities and limitations of being a lover in the subcontinent.

Looking

I met him on my way to Gangtok. A boy from Darjeeling. His parents have moved to Siliguri. The hills are harsh for the old, I guess. *Boredom*, he replied. We spoke about tennis, the World Cup and Kolkata. He liked my city for reasons that I couldn't understand. Their Gorkhaland scuttled with notes and shells. Another occupied Kashmir perhaps. He helped me get a taxi before leaving. // *I am Rajorshi. You are?* I forgot his name. Like I always do. This is a nation of selective amnesia. He had told me that he plays … sings actually… at Gangtok Groove. *I've heard of another place that plays rock.* He nodded, a little embarrassed. *I mentioned Groove because I play there. There are many such.* // I went to that café in the evening. No one was playing. *We'll have music tomorrow*, they said. I went the next day, to heal my bitter disappointment. Long hair is dangerous. *You look like a terrorist, chop off your hair*, they advised near Nathu-La with the promise of a pass next time. // I walk in. He isn't there. He had

223

said he will come on Saturday but I was hoping. *Will you stay for the music? You'll have to pay.* They asked me thrice. I felt drained. *Do you know this guy from Darjeeling who comes here to sing? His name starts with an 'O' I think. Is there anyone? Only a cook.* Oh // I finished my salad and drink. The woman across from me ordered the same. She wore an expensive perfume. *Can you lend me a pen?* I wrote a message and my number. *Give this to him ... if you find him. Maybe you'll remember a guy like that. Please.* Maybe he too will remember and ask.

DIA B.

Dianthe (pronounced dye-ann-thee) is a mathématicienne in training. She and her fellow goblins live in a tree, write poetry and invoke old magic to pass the time. She is trans and bisexual, and hopes to be less scared of bigots one day.

Submission

To remit unto another
oneself or what one possesses

> Possess is a funny word
> to give to a body so politicized
> to a body so conflicted
> that it looks to its own scars
> with gratefulness

I say it
not he or she or them
those are for the person inside this body

> But the body itself
> is the thing
> upon which the politics of personhood

are inflicted
     yet it is its most
     uncontrollable cog

  A body
wrenching, writhing
with unbounded desire
  A body
pathologized, taxonomized
made symmetrical
to fit a curriculum

'Taxonomy is taxidermy,' a sister tells me
from her perch

     Unto ourselves, us taxidermists' prizes
     us butterflies nailed to boards
     She speaks like a hammer
     my dear, dear sister

For it is so well understood
'society must be defended'
knowledge must stay sacred
the body must be bound.

TANNI

Tanni is a migrant Bengali small-town ciswoman. She found the words asexuality and Cultural Studies with some help and hasn't looked back since. She is awaiting the evaluation of her doctoral thesis on intersectionality and identity while working as a researcher, teacher, editor and translator. Social media makes her anxious.

Billeting

Within the cozy comfort
of our lives in closets
(we are ingenious, privileged,
creative even) we have
beddings, and boxes
of family albums and
a fully appointed kitchen, and
the technique to balance
being the daughter, sister,
granddaughter, the orphaned
Materfamilias of orphans.
Yet we keep a corner
of our selves packed
neatly away in the safe
warmth and cool shade of

the marriage behind the
doors
looking
pretty
efficient
useful – all the promises
of adulthood
coming true.

Then someone peeks in,
smiles with the
indulgence I have grown
to hate, and says:
'Aren't you a bit too
old/overqualified/womanly
for slumber parties with
best friends?'

SNEHASHISH DAS

Poet Snehashish Das, a Bahujan person, has been a part of Ambedkarite politics in fighting multi-layered oppression through activism, academia, poetry, dance and art. Snehashish ceases to identify with the boxes of gender and sex. Buddhist consciousness helped them unlearn caste and gender, and learn the truth of body i.e. impermanence.

Everyone says

Everyone says
this dupatta cannot be mine,
then why does it shine
so beautiful on my shoulder?
Why, when it grazes against my waist,
does a rose of youth bloom on my body,
in my mind?

When I'd gone to find a dupatta,
I had my eyes only for this one.
Only this one had the right to choose
its own colour. I asked the shopkeeper:
how much? He said 'two twenty',
'and for me?'

He just stared, said
'Everything'.

My mother doesn't like this dupatta.
The shame of my home
shines in its creases.
Between the honour of homes
and this dupatta, how do we choose?
For years my caste refused,
rebelled, fought for respect, how
could a dupatta bring them shame?
Why is a battle aflame
between honour and disgrace
in the folds of my dupatta?

This saffron dupatta, friends say,
doesn't suit my dark body.
When a slight breeze moves it
from my waist, that childhood scar
– I never had the courage to erase,
which bears the stain of my
pains and joys that had been –
suddenly it can be seen.
Should I keep this scar
or wear this dupatta;
the choice, I resist.

This dupatta is a flag
of my self-assuredness, of my guts,
it has taken me years to plant it

firmly to the ground. But since when have
we ever been allowed guts? How dare we
be brave? Then how can this dupatta
be ours, be mine? The retribution
for this crime, can we survive?

I know I am not permitted the dream
of draping it. But today there's only
my scream, my claim that this is mine.
I know they will laugh
but I will gulp down all cruelty,
all rebukes, everything that they can say.
I know the cost of liberation,
maybe now I'm ready to pay.

Translated from the Hindi by Snehashish Das & Akhil Katyal

Poet's note: The colour saffron, used here, is a political choice by me to reclaim
this colour as a Buddhist symbol and as a representation of the truth of body
and life, from negative connotations Hinduism has attached to it.

RIYA GHOSH RAY

Riya Ghosh Ray has been living in Delhi on and off for the past nine years. She recently finished her MPhil and is currently working in a not-for-profit organization. She divides her time working, writing, rewriting, making paper boats and waiting for the rain.

Dirty Laundry

I was sixteen. Just another teenage girl whose Facebook and Orkut reeked of such sentimentality that it got easy to discard her as just another emotional little bitch, wasting away her life after yet another dick. The small-town asked me to solve my problems inside, wash the dirty laundry inside. No one wants to see me. I stopped talking at all. You too asked me to wash my dirty laundry inside my dirty home. Because dirty laundry is to be washed at home. Or, you pay your psychiatrist to clean it for you like you do at the dhobi mart next door. Then you walk out with a pile of clean clothes. Like her smelly lipstick never stained it. Like no blood was spilled on account of nothing and then almost everything, every night. Like you never sat in the muddy waters of your own piss and tears by the telephone, contemplating whether you should call the police before or after one of your parents, most likely your mother, dies. Wait and wash. Then repeat. Till your laundry gets so piled up, so dirty, that you now need to call for outside help to get it cleaned.

Drag the dirt out only to bury it so deep that you can never unearth your mother's experiences, almost never get flowers to her dreaded memories. That's how you'll deal with it. You'll keep the streets clean and never talk about the girl you loved. You had signed an agreement that whatever is there between us is dirt and had solemnly vowed not to bring it to the streets. I know you don't have the strength for it. Don't shed tears over people who left you in a haste before you could even contemplate free-falling. It makes you seem like a slimy, creepy, weakling crawling across streets shouting for attention. It is better to cry under blankets. Press your head inside the pillow as if doing so would transfer all your anger onto the bed and warm it up for a goodnight's sleep. You can always wash the pillow case the next morning. Don't lash out now. You are going to get ashamed from dirtying the public place if you do so. Your experience is for your pubic space, keep the public space clean. You get infected by your own dirt, perish and eventually die. The streets remain clean. You sleep in filth. Invisible. Shivering in constant anxiety and panic attacks. And when I decide to say it out loud, under a spotlight they say, 'very brave' or miss the whole point and call it fiction, 'very good, very much into the character' or pat me on the back and say, 'make something beautiful out of your misery, poetry!' or the clichéd, 'wow! That was depressing, wow!' My poems are not supposed to make you feel good because I know love as revolt and not fantasised romance. I am ugly and I hope that the poems I give birth to are monsters enough to torment you. My misery is enough, it won't turn into anything else. But my invisibility cloak succeeds. All. The. Time. It is sometimes strong enough to send you home with a sigh of relief. With the self-congratulatory smile on your face because you cleaned your home spot-free inside-out, how no one hushed you, because violence got so normalised that you never talked about it. Rather you would come in here talk some blues, about love and peace, how we are all one with no differences like the Dylan-Lennon cover boy – Feel Good. I feel bad. I'll paint my dirt on the streets because you did paint it all over me. Silent and fast and in secret that it did not even give me a chance to scream. I'll keep slamming your faces with this dirt, till you recognise that the dirt belongs to you too. Till my bravery, my desperation to go incognito breaks down, and I finally get to be scared and fragile. Till you understand that I do not hurt myself because I hate myself. It's because I cannot slap you across your face. And mostly because, I am tired of washing my dirty laundry in private yielding to you, only beauty.

SIMPLE RAJRAH

Simple Rajrah is an MPhil student at the University of Oxford. She has formerly completed her post graduate studies at Jawaharlal Nehru University and undergraduate studies at University of Delhi.

Jasdeep Singh is a translator, screenwriter and software engineer. He has written dialogues for critically acclaimed Punjabi films *Annhe Ghore Da Daan* and *Chauthi Koot*. He curates *Parchanve*, a blog on translated Punjabi literature and co-curates *Kirrt*, a visual archive of Punjabi labour.

What do I not buy

What is this?
Ice.
I ran bare foot, searched like the mad do; Why didn't you come for the last time?
I pined beyond measure; come, put one slab on my soul.

What is this?
Sand.
I am not a mausoleum, what do I need these tiny pebbles for?
Yes, but the corpse of my desires lies there, empty the full sack on it.

What is this?

Salt.

Traded-off, when we had to flee from Rattowal (that Punjab) to
Nawanshehar (this Punjab).

If you got it from the same woman put it in my mouth.

What is this?

Rain.

We got the house from the Muslims, but we kept the pir's shrine in
the backyard intact.

If the raindrops are washed from the mazaar get them close to my
chest.

What is this?

Fog.

Whether from Lahore or Jammu, it won't tell you what lies ahead.

If it is the chill from her moist hands, stitch it in my hair.

Translated from the Pothohaari Punjabi by Jasdeep Singh with the author

DIA M. YONZON

Dia is a law graduate specializing International Human Rights Law and works as a researcher in LGBT+/Queer Rights. Dia writes and performs spoken word poetry for their friends and family, *mostly* related to their queer experiences.

To the Fish
You Don't Know How To Swim

Do you remember the summer, reading by the pool when your siblings were already inside the water?

Or the time, you went for a hike with your friends, your sun-beaten body eased when you heard the sound of the spring.

Both times, you wanted nothing more than to merge your body, deep down under –

you didn't.

You wanted nothing more than to feel the cold water on your bare skin. You couldn't.

Your toes under water. But your head already drowning.

Have you learned to ride the waves of your own imagining?

Have you learned to appreciate the effervescence, slowly leaving your body – gasping?

Remember, when the tides get scary, to push the water back with your hands.

Remember, your feet are not tied to the rock at the bottom.

PITAMBAR NAIK

Pitambar Naik is a poet, writer and activist from western Odisha in India. He believes Hindutva is the Indian version of fascism and casteism is the mother to all evils in India that must be annihilated. He has been published in almost ten countries, has a book of poems *The Anatomy of Solitude*, and is currently working on a second collection.

Banavasi Dhangadamajhi

Banavasi Dangadamajhi is a geographical ambiguity
his name is a cultural, bipolar hashtag
he's flatly eclipsed and anonymously addressed

his identity is wrapped in history's arcane chapters –
a civilization's anathema
his story could make no Netflix tragedy.
What's the hypothesis of Indian history?
Is it anything more than
a cricket inning or a *Puspak Viman*?

A dream swings like tenacity
like the promise of a weaver bird
like a restless curvature
and the wobbling rhythm of honey bees,

every evening, the folk songs spiral
the architecture of *mahua* bear and *rangabati*
for a sweet juxtaposition.
To forget its sensibility
the moon drinks its snowy glitz.

The dear ones sit around the happy hearth and talk,
laughter spills over bags of millet
sweetening the pain,
the map of a million mutinies
knits hope bit by bit
to share the Eucharist of commonality.

There's a deluge of acrimony
along the Chhatisgarh borders,
a flock of opponents sucks bones
the hunger-hit sun and polio-smitten life at Bongomunda,
a little above his palm lines, the Dangadamajhi's sky
flies a corollary half-truth
and an old model of a Boeing jet.

The margin of pain tries hard to breathe a new climax
waiting and seeking
grappling to giggle at a tender frond
to pluck a few petals of the decaying dusk
the allegory of an afternoon twangs like a pendulum
the deprived yawn of Banavasi Dhangadamajhi
looks for a divine Canaan.

BHASKAR MAJUMDER

Bhaskar Majumder is a school teacher by profession. He has published a book of poetry (*Heyro Abeger Gunitawk*) and a Bengali translation of Hansda Sowvendra Shekhar's *The Mysterious Ailment of Rupi Baskey*. He did his masters in English language and literature. He is gay and lives in Kolkata.

Souradeep Roy is a translator, poet, and performer currently based in Delhi.

Baban-da and Stars in the Sky

Because I slowly shifted my weight on your tummy sitting in front of
   your cycle
you had thrown me into the soft grass.
Those days I had likened your tummy to stars in the sky.
They were the nineties, bazaar-economy, and I was then in class six.
Because you wanted to study in that Purulia ashram
it was easy for you to leave me.
I'm not a woman after all!
How I kept staring at the light in the study-table;
no one cared to ask how I was.
I couldn't figure out why I felt I'm carrying a brick on my chest all
   the time.

Trying to forget you I stood second in my class.
But adolescence is not a time for amnesia.
Nor is it a time when we are thrifty about tears.
Now when I see your photos
with your wife and son
I feel I have the right to sleep on your tummy.
I still think it's a constellation of stars.

I have grown up.

Translated from the Bengali by Souradeep Roy

SHAIKH MD. MOMINUL ISLAM

Born in Khulna, Bangladesh, Shaikh Md. Mominul Islam is a gay man, an LGBTIQA+/Queer rights and Human rights activist. He is the founder of Vivid Rainbow LGBT community and a member of South Asian queer Youth Activists' Network (SAYAN). He designed the Bangladeshi Pride Flag. A writer and teacher, Mominul is an ex-Muslim, Eco-Feminist & Marxist.

Shikhandi's Complaint

I couldn't forget you when I wanted to;
couldn't even erase you
from the pages of my memory.
How can I, tell me?
You have, after all,
left such bright scars inside me
and gone away;
can I cure them simply because I want to?
I had surrendered everything to you:
my mind, my life-breath, body, soul, my entire domestic world;
I had placed you in the place reserved for my household gods
risking my entire being!
And after the puja, you were so negligent:
you left me, you went away.

And yet, and yet, I accepted your negligence,
filled my heart with the left-over prasad!
I don't know which flower I should have recited mantras to
for you to be sufficiently satisfied.
Now that you are not satisfied
I don't want to worship you anymore.
I am now a rebellious 'shaitan'
expelled from your heaven.
No, I don't want the suffocating pleasures
of such a heaven.
I am happier in this suffering hell.
And I don't want anyone's compassion,
don't want to hear a sympathetic
'Dear o dear' from anyone.
Now I am heartless, I am a stone!
Now I can forget you for long spells;
I don't hesitate sharing the bed
with another man;
I feel like I am a prostitute from the street.
But it's better
than being chaste.
What was the value of my chastity?
Now I want to remain a prostitute.
What do you care?
When you threw away the flowers for the puja
on that morning so negligently,
you did not even turn to see
who stepped over them.
I want to forget you but I can't.

Please, please, dear o'dear,
release me from this moh-maya!
'Dear God! What kind of curse
have you given!
In my next life, send me back
like a complete "man" or a complete "woman"!'
Then I will also show you
how happy I am!

Translated from the Bengali by Souradeep Roy

KIRAN TOLIYA

In Kiran's own words, 'I don't know what identity to give myself. I am an unfulfilled dream, yet peerless. I am a transman. I like girls. It has taken me years to find myself, to find comfort. Vikalp (in Gujarat) has been helpful for me. It's true, there is no *vilkalp* (alternative) for Vikalp.'

I keep searching for a self

somewhere in me
lost, feeling for my way
somewhere in me
thoughts clamour, battles rage
somewhere in me
a confusion festers
somewhere in me
where should I go
whom should I tell
that I am lost, relentlessly
somewhere in me
faith still burns, survives
one day, somewhere in the world
an upheaval, a churn
that day the way it thinks

will turn
it will know
what I am
        where I breathe
somewhere in me

Translated from the Gujarati by Dhiren Borisa

CHANDINI

Chandini was 'born in a Dalit family as a boy but was yearning to be a woman'. Founding member of Payana and a longstanding activist in the field of human rights and HIV health, she is an award-winning poet and her work is taught at several universities. Working in the corporate sector for a decade now, in Three Wheels United, she is currently writing her autobiography.

Ajji's Death and Mahadevappa

When Ajji died
unable to answer those around,
Appa made a big ruckus
disowning his daughter who wasn't a son,
Banning me from participating in the death ceremony.
My hues and cries failed to knock the door to his heart.
It was all about the pride of his family lineage.

At Appa's death ritual, when I the daughter
decided to sacrifice my beautiful long hair
and shave my head
the family stopped me
by opening their arms of acceptance.

As Appa wished, for a family with no lineage;
I became a mother, then
a support to my mother.

Translated from the Kannada by Mamta Sagar

Translator's note: Mahadevappa is poet Chandini's father's name; 'Ajji' is grandmother in the Kannada; according to Hindu death rituals, sons (who are considered the bearers of family lineage) shave their heads when parents die.

Ahalye

Ayyo! in pain I say,
Hogalo ... out you go says them

Preeti in love I say
Ja re ... they shun me away

in hope I look at them
grief is what they give

Those that I longed were so different
Those here are dissimilar from that

Longing for a change in perspectives
I wait here like a stone.

Translated from the Kannada by Mamta Sagar

Translator's note: Ahalye is a mythological character from the Ramayana. She is
the wife of Rishi Gautama. Seduced by Indra and then cursed by her husband
for infidelity, she is turned into stone. Ahalye waits for Rama to liberate her
from the curse.

RAMCHANDRA SRINIVAS SIRAS

Ramchandra Siras (1948–2010) was a poet and Professor of Marathi Literature at Aligarh Muslim University. On 8 February 2010, two men forced their way into Dr Siras's house and shot a video of him in bed with another man. The next day, Siras was suspended for 'gross misconduct'. The Courts ruled against the university. In April that year, Dr Siras died in a rented house under mysterious circumstances, a day before the official letter revoking his suspension arrived.

Anish Gawande is a writer and translator. He is the director of the Dara Shikoh Fellowship and the founder of The Pink List. Gawande graduated with a degree in comparative literature and society from Columbia University and is currently a Rhodes Scholar pursuing a degree in intellectual history at Oxford University.

Rooms to sleep in

He's already bathed in sweat,
it's very hot, after all.
He shows me – work of his dreams
completed just today – beyond
are rooms to sleep in.

When this house lay unbuilt,
no money and no constraints

251

of diktats of the previous owner's
incomplete dreams, I told him
– don't block the mountains with windows
or walls, even – let them come right in
into the house, not like guests
but family.

But his obstinate, mad love for solitude
wants not flowers on the steps below
wants not tunes in middle octaves –
here, only those rooms to sleep in,
only those were built
for a purpose.

There, wind, silence, softness
and that *parvana* of easy dream-journeys
wants not magical colours
and unfiltered compositions of sunlight
and drawers to keep sleeping pills.

He has built for himself
– for what remains of his life –
a grave as beautiful
as epiphanies, he calls it
rooms to sleep in.

Translated from the Marathi by Anish Gawande

ACKNOWLEDGEMENTS

It didn't take a village, it took a country or two. Or three. Many people have made this anthology possible. They have helped us, in the root sense of *anthology*, to gather (*legein*) its flowers (*anthos*).

Sohini Basak, the commissioning editor of this book, is a miracle. She has seen it evolve for over two years. She was full of ideas, resourceful with translators, patient with our timelines, pragmatic with suggestions, and might as well be the third editor of this book, if the amount of work is anything to go by. We thank her profusely.

Many, many people helped us spread the call, put us in touch with potential contributors, stepped in to translate the poems, gave us ideas, corrected our mistakes, and encouraged us (literally *gave us courage*) through more than a year it took to put together this book. To each of them we owe a lot.

Dhiren Borisa stepped in to translate the Gujarati poem despite his tight schedule. Mamta Sagar translated the Kannada poems despite hers. Further, she got us Rumi's powerful poem. Karthik Bittu Kondaiah and Gee Semmalar put us in touch with Chandini. The lovely folks at Roopbaan in Bangladesh circulated the call, so did our friends in Queeristan in Pakistan. Mirak Raheem in Sri Lanka did the same. The poet Chandramohan S. told us about Vijayarajamallika's work in Malayalam. Anish Gawande and we searched for Dr Siras's book *Paya Khalchi Hirawal* together and he gave us a wonderful translation of one of its poems. Ash Kotak was both super kind and resourceful in putting us in touch with several queer poets. Minal Hajratwala was generous with her suggestions. The activist Ramki L Ramakrishnan *tagged* several folks when the call first started floating, including Santa Khurai, who contributed. Vebhuti Duggal helped us translate the call into Hindi, Jenny Bhatt into Gujarati, Shalini Annie and Mydhili MS into Malayalam, Kavitha Muralidharan into Tamil, Abdur Rehman Khan into Urdu. Thanks are also due to Souradeep Roy and Rohan Chettri for helping us with translations last minute. There are many more such folks without whose wishes and work this book would have had half of its scope and a quarter of its strength.

Many conversations with the poets Vqueeram Aditya Sahai and Aditi Rao helped us thresh through what this anthology could be, what the challenges of putting it together are like, what its promise was, what its possible lapses were. Any of the latter, of course, are entirely ours.

Ruth Vanita, Saleem Kidwai, Hoshang Merchant, Ashwini Sukthankar, Minal Hajratwala, all authors and anthologists extraordinaire, paved the road for an anthology like ours. If it hadn't been for their work, it would be difficult to imagine such a book. Their editorial efforts and writings make the history, to which this book is a small addition.

Some of the poems in this anthology have been previously published in print books, journals and online magazines. Our gratitude to the editors and publishers. Ruth Vanita's 'Garment' from *Another Country: An Anthology of Post-Independence Indian Poetry in English* ed. Arundhati Subramanian (New Delhi: Sahitya Akademi, 2013); Minal Hajratwala's 'Incantation for the Occasion' in *Feminist Studies* and 'Ghazal' in *Weber Studies*; Vikram Seth's 'Across' and 'All Those Who Sleep Tonight' in *All Those Who Sleep Tonight* (New Delhi: Penguin Books India, 1990); Rajiv Mohabir's 'Inside the Belly' in *Killer Whale Journal* and 'Interpreting Behaviour' in *Southern Humanities Review*; Hoshang Merchant's 'My Sister Takes a Long Time to Die' in *My Sunset Marriage* (New Delhi: Navayana, 2016) and 'Sind' in *Sufiana: Poems* (New Delhi: HaperCollins India, 2013); Fatimah Asghar's 'Pluto Shits on the Universe' in *Poetry* journal; Sreshtha's 'The Sonneteer Gets a Heartbreaker's Haircut' in *Glass Poetry* and 'This Is Not Yet Another Poem About My Mother' in *The Margins*; Karuna Chandrasekhar's 'Translation/Delhi: a love story' on *Anomalylit* and 'aftermath' on *Rising Phoenix Review*; Aqdas Aftab's 'All Death' in *Yes Poetry*; Kazim Ali's 'Exit strategy' on the Academy of American Poets' *Poem-a-Day* website; Leah Lakshmi Piepzna-Samarasinha's 'Parliaments on the Stoop' in *Room Magazine*; Orooj-e-Zafar's 'My Sister, by Land' in *Desi Writers' Lounge*; Sultan Padamsee's 'O Pomponia Mine!' in *Poems* (Kolkata: Writer's Workshop, 1975); Amal Rana's 'Janazah for Pulse' in *Glass Poetry*; Hadi Hussain's 'Fat Talk' on the tumblr blog *It Gets Fatter*; Akhil Katyal's 'When Farida Khanum' in How Many Countries Does the Indus Cross (New Delhi: TGIPC, 2019). Every effort was made to trace the copyright holder for each poem and its translation. For any that might have been inadvertently omitted, the publishers would be happy to make the necessary amendments.